ANOINTING
FALL *on* ME

ACCESSING THE POWER
OF THE HOLY SPIRIT

T.D. Jakes

DESTINY IMAGE® PUBLISHERS, INC.

P.O. Box 310, Shippensburg, PA 17257-0310

"Publishing cutting-edge prophetic resources to supernaturally empower the body of Christ"

This book and all other Destiny Image and Destiny Image Fiction books are available at Christian bookstores and distributors worldwide.

For more information on foreign distributors, call 717-532-3040.

Reach us on the Internet: www.destinyimage.com.

ISBN 13 TP: 978-0-7684-7208-0
ISBN 13 eBook: 978-0-7684-7209-7
ISBN 13 HC: 978-0-7684-7211-0
ISBN 13 LP: 978-0-7684-7210-3

For Worldwide Distribution, Printed in the USA
1 2 3 4 5 6 7 8 / 27 26 25 24 23

CONTENTS

PREFACE FROM PUBLISHER

A *nointing Fall On Me* was one of the first Christian books I read by choice. I had been brought up in a nominal Christian environment, receiving religious education. In those situations, however, the books I read were not by choice; they were assignments that my school grades depended on.

But *Anointing Fall on Me* was a book that started to instrumentally form my theology of and relationship with a real person called the Holy Spirit. Bishop T.D. Jakes refers to Him as the *Holy Ghost* in this original text of the book, and truthfully, I wanted to keep it *as is*. Why?

I received my Master of Divinity in Church History and Renewal, with a particular emphasis in Pentecostal history. In times past, there was an expectation that when the *Holy Ghost* was moving, *something* was truly happening. When the *Holy Ghost* showed up, there would be evidence. When the *Holy Ghost* came upon you, you would absolutely know it and you would never be the same.

For the days ahead, whether you are a pastor or middle school principal, whether you are a business-person or boat captain, whether you are a stay-at-home parent raising children or a doctor, you need the wisdom, presence, and supernatural power of the Holy Spirit to infuse your life. Apart from Him you can do nothing. He is the Spirit of Jesus; He is God Almighty with you 24/7.

We need to go back to these cornerstones of the faith: the Holy Spirit and His anointing. They are not exclusive property of one denomination; they are the inheritance of every single believer.

LARRY SPARKS
Publisher of Destiny Image

FOREWORD

I cannot think of a greater living example of the consistent ability to draw on the anointing of the Lord. T.D. Jakes is a man without equal. There is much we can all learn from his words, his spirit, and his passion in delivering the Word of the Lord. Just watching him is a wonder in itself. The Presence of the Lord flows so freely from him as he teaches. He is simple, clear, and honest in his delivery. Sometimes urgent, sometimes gentle, but always accurate and penetrating. He is a man whose inner focus is on the Lord Himself. Even in his most emotional presentation, you can also see the rest and peace in his eyes.

The Holy Spirit will always move freely through those who have no other desire than to give the word of the Lord to hungry people. And make no mistake about it, God has much to say to His people. He has much He wants to communicate to the world around us. There is much to learn from the bishop's words, but also his method, his passion, and his love of the Lord Jesus Himself.

I first met the bishop at a small conference in the Pocono Mountains where he was ministering. That was just before he wrote *Woman, Thou Art Loosed.* We literally walked into each other that fateful afternoon in the basement area of the conference center where vendors were displaying their products. The moment I touched him, I prophesied about a book churning in his heart. A few weeks later he called me and the rest, as they say, is history.

There are three criteria we use when determining the possibility of publishing a new author. We look at the person, his message, and his ministry. In the bishop's case, all three were intricately wrapped with integrity, gentleness, and truth.

We are proud to offer this work to the world.

T.D. Jakes is a man who has allowed the Lord to mold him into a vessel He can use to change the lives of millions around the world. We are grateful to be a part of God's plan for the life of Bishop T.D. Jakes.

DON NORI SR.
Founder, Destiny Image Publishers

INTRODUCTION

I feel compelled to present scriptural truth on the Holy Ghost that is simple, timely, and applicable to your life. I believe this is a very timely book—one that will equip you to meet the devil's end-time onslaught to thwart the plan of God.

I believe that we're in the beginning stages of the greatest revival this world has ever known. In order for us to carry out the plan of God, we must realize that divine intervention and not human effort will usher in this end-time revival. Christians must know that their lives with God can be full of new experiences every day. Instead of merely enduring our salvation, we can enjoy the fullness that God has provided in the Holy Ghost.

If you have been saved by the grace of God, you have a calling on your life. God may want you to be a pastor, an evangelist, or a missionary. He may call you to be a light in the business world. You may have been apprehended by the hand of God to write books, lead people in worship, or raise godly children.

You need to realize that these gifts and callings were not placed in your life to lie dormant. Only by the power of the Holy Ghost will you see them fulfilled. This book will show you how to meet challenges and realize your full potential.

If you apply these practical truths in your life, you will begin to experience a new freshness in God. The plans that you have hoped to fulfill all your life will become reality. Do you long for certain things in God? Does your sanctified soul stir at the thought of doing exploits for God? A sense of destiny causes you to determine, "No matter what I must go through, I can and will make it!"

These truths on the Holy Ghost will take you to higher heights and deeper depths in God. Get ready to experience a new joy and power that will change your life—and the lives of others.

CHAPTER 1

ASK, SEEK, KNOCK

One of the greatest controversies in all the Bible concerns the Godhead.

"Hear, O Israel: The Lord our God is one Lord" (Deut. 6:4).

If there is one God, as Scripture teaches, how can there be a Son who says that He and His Father are one? If there is only one God, how can there be *"three that bear record in heaven, the Father, the Word, and the Holy Ghost: and these three are one"* (1 John 5:7).

The concept of the Godhead is a mystery that has baffled Christians for years. With our limited minds we try to comprehend a limitless God. How can we explain one God but three distinct manifestations? Some have used the analogy of ice, water, and steam being the same in substance but differing according to temperature. Others have shown how one man can be a father, a husband, and a son at the same time.

While we may never completely understand the Godhead, Scripture teaches that our lives can be tremendously impacted by the present ministry of the Holy Ghost. The first step is welcoming, or receiving, the power of the Holy Ghost.

You Can Receive the Holy Ghost

You have the right to receive the Holy Ghost because Jesus prayed for you to receive Him.

> *And I will pray the Father, and he shall give you another Comforter, that he may abide with you for ever* (John 14:16).

The Greek word for Comforter, *parakletos,* means "one called alongside to help, to defend as an attorney." It also means "another one just like me." The same word means "advocate" in this Scripture:

> *My little children, these things write I unto you, that ye sin not. And if any man sin, we have an advocate with the Father, Jesus Christ the righteous* (1 John 2:1).

Christ is our advocate in Heaven; the Holy Ghost is our advocate on earth.

The Holy Ghost has been given to assist us in a variety of ways. He helps to guide us:

> *Howbeit when he, the Spirit of truth, is come, he will guide you into all truth: for he shall not speak of himself; but whatsoever he shall hear, that shall he speak: and he will shew you things to come* (John 16:13).

He assures us that we are children of God:

> *The Spirit itself beareth witness with our spirit, that we are the children of God* (Romans 8:16).

He gives us power to witness:

> *But ye shall receive power, after that the Holy Ghost is come upon you: and ye shall be witnesses unto me both in Jerusalem, and in all Judaea, and in Samaria, and unto the uttermost part of the earth* (Acts 1:8).

He helps us to pray:

> *Likewise the Spirit also helpeth our infirmities: for we know not what we should pray for as we ought: but the Spirit itself maketh intercession for us with groanings which cannot be uttered* (Romans 8:26).

He enables us to bear the fruit of the Spirit:

But the fruit of the Spirit is love, joy, peace, longsuffering, gentleness, goodness, faith, meekness, temperance: against such there is no law (Galatians 5:22-23).

The Holy Ghost is always present. He is our backup!

The Holy Ghost is our backup!

While Jesus was departing, He prayed that another One just like Him would come. That One is the Holy Ghost. The Holy Ghost would stand by the children of God to assist them in carrying out the same work—and even "greater works":

Verily, verily, I say unto you, He that believeth on me, the works that I do shall he do also; and greater works than these shall he do; because I go unto my Father (John 14:12).

Believers must understand the ministry of the Holy Ghost so they can carry out the will of God for their lives.

We aren't alone when we lie down at night or go through the storms of life. When we go through a valley or through a trial, the Holy Ghost is there to defend us. God will never leave us nor forsake us (Heb. 13:5). Jesus is with us to the end of this age (Matt. 28:20). When we receive the fullness of the Holy Ghost, we receive an eternal friend. Jesus is praying that you have an intimate relationship with the Holy Ghost.

Many friends stay with us until we mess up or until we disagree with them. They quickly leave as if they never knew us. But the Holy Ghost, our Comforter, stays with us forever.

The Holy Ghost does not come and go based upon the circumstances of our lives. He is there when we do well; He is there when we fail. When we are on top of things, He is there. When things are on top of us, He is there. No matter what the situation, the Holy Ghost is always there to help us. In the same way that Jesus helped the disciples, the Holy Ghost now helps us.

When Do We Receive the Holy Ghost?

This controversial question has been debated for years. God's Word shows that a person receives the Holy Ghost as a mark of identity, confirming that he or she really is a child of God (John 3:5-6; Rom. 8:9,14-16; Gal. 4:6). Jesus told His disciples that the world (unbelievers) could not receive the Holy Ghost because it "seeth Him not" (John 14:17).

Scripture also shows us, however, that receiving the Holy Ghost at salvation is not the same as being filled with the Holy Ghost. Some disciples followed Jesus for years and only later were filled with the Holy

Ghost and spoke with other tongues as the Spirit gave them utterance.

> *And, behold, I send the promise of my Father upon you: but tarry ye in the city of Jerusalem, until ye be endued with power from on high (Luke 24:49).*

> *In the last day, that great day of the feast, Jesus stood and cried, saying, If any man thirst, let him come unto me, and drink. He that believeth on me, as the scripture hath said, out of his belly shall flow rivers of living water. (But this spake he of the Spirit, which they that believe on him should receive: for the Holy Ghost was not yet given; because that Jesus was not yet glorified) (John 7:37-39).*

> *Therefore being by the right hand of God exalted, and having received of the Father the promise of the Holy Ghost, he hath shed forth this, which ye now see and hear. For David is not ascended into the heavens: but he saith himself, The Lord said unto my Lord, Sit thou on my right hand, until I make thy foes thy footstool. Therefore let all the house of Israel know assuredly, that God hath made the same Jesus, whom ye have crucified, both Lord and Christ. Now when they heard this, they were pricked in their heart, and said*

*unto Peter and to the rest of the apostles, Men
and brethren, what shall we do? Then Peter
said unto them, Repent, and be baptized
every one of you in the name of Jesus Christ
for the remission of sins, and ye shall receive
the gift of the Holy Ghost. For the promise
is unto you, and to your children, and to all
that are afar off, even as many as the Lord
our God shall call* (Acts 2:33-39).

*And we are his witnesses of these things; and
so is also the Holy Ghost, whom God hath
given to them that obey him* (Acts 5:32).

*Christ hath redeemed us from the curse of
the law, being made a curse for us: for it is
written, Cursed is every one that hangeth on
a tree: that the blessing of Abraham might
come on the Gentiles through Jesus Christ;
that we might receive the promise of the Spirit
through faith* (Galatians 3:13-14).

You can be saved, but not necessarily filled or baptized with the Holy Ghost. We receive the Holy Ghost as a mark of identity when we are saved, but another experience—the baptism in the Holy Ghost—awaits us.

*While Peter yet spake these words, the Holy
Ghost fell on all them which heard the word.*

And they of the circumcision which believed were astonished, as many as came with Peter, because that on the Gentiles also was poured out the gift of the Holy Ghost. For they heard them speak with tongues, and magnify God (Acts 10:44-46).

And it came to pass, that, while Apollos was at Corinth, Paul having passed through the upper coasts came to Ephesus: and finding certain disciples, he said unto them, Have ye received the Holy Ghost since ye believed? And they said unto him, We have not so much as heard whether there be any Holy Ghost. And he said unto them, Unto what then were ye baptized? And they said, Unto John's baptism. Then said Paul, John verily baptized with the baptism of repentance, saying unto the people, that they should believe on him which should come after him, that is, on Christ Jesus. When they heard this, they were baptized in the name of the Lord Jesus. And when Paul had laid his hands upon them, the Holy Ghost came on them; and they spake with tongues, and prophesied. And all the men were about twelve (Acts 19:1-7).

The believers in these verses had not been baptized in or received the infilling of the Holy Ghost.

The apostle Paul commanded the Ephesian believers to *"be filled with the Spirit"* (Eph. 5:18). They had already been saved by the grace of God (Eph. 2:8-9) and had been sealed by the Holy Ghost (Eph. 1:13). They had been positionally placed in the heavenlies with Christ Jesus (Eph. 2:6). They had become His workmanship (Eph. 2:10). They had been blessed with every spiritual blessing, chosen before the foundation of the world, and predestined to be adopted by Jesus Christ (Eph. 1:3-5).

Despite all these things, the apostle Paul admonished them to be filled with the Holy Ghost. He did not merely suggest that the saints receive the infilling of the Holy Ghost, he commanded them to do so!

> *The apostle Paul commanded the saints to receive the Holy Ghost.*

To make his point, the apostle Paul issued two commandments: *"Be not drunk with wine"* and *"Be ye filled with the Spirit"* (Eph. 5:18). He used a negative command, something we should not do, to accentuate something that we should do.

Being "drunk with wine" means that we are intoxicated or under the control of wine. To be drunk means that you have given yourself over to the alcohol. In order to remain drunk, one must continue to partake of whatever brought about the drunkenness.

Paul knew the saints would never come to church or attempt any type of service for the Lord while under the influence of wine. But if it were wrong to be drunk on wine and attempt to serve God, then it would be equally wrong to attempt to serve God and not be filled or intoxicated with the Holy Ghost.

When a person is drunk, he or she becomes a totally different person. Drunks become very bold, even fearless, as their emotions are overtaken by the wine. Their speech is often slurred, and their walk is unsteady.

In order for the Ephesians to be happy and bold, to walk in the will of God, to talk in a new way, and not be afraid of their future, they needed to be filled with the Holy Ghost.

Next, the apostle Paul focused on the home, dealing with the relationship between husbands and wives and between parents and their children.

Ephesians closes with a discussion of the battle that we face as children of God. If we are to partake of the blessings that God has predestined for us, if we are to be the workmanship of God, if we are to enjoy a happy marriage and rear children in the fear and admonition of the Lord, we will face a spiritual battle. Living a Spirit-filled life, however, abundantly equips us to carry out these tasks.

Passover Must Precede Pentecost

The nation of Israel recognized many feasts, but we will only focus on Passover and Pentecost. While these two feasts were primarily for Israel, we can make some dynamic secondary applications for the church.

Passover had been recognized by Israel since their departure from the land of Egypt.

God commanded the elders of the nation of Israel to kill a lamb and apply its blood to the two side posts and the overhead lintel of the door of every house. That night, God sent a death angel throughout Egypt to slay the firstborn of every household. When He saw the blood over the doorposts of the Israelites, however, He promised to pass over them and not execute the same judgment that befell the Egyptians (Exod. 12).

This is a type of Jesus who is our Passover Lamb (1 Cor. 5:7). Through His death and shed blood, we have been accepted by God. Seeing the blood of Christ, our substitute, God has passed over us and withheld judgment for our sins.

The time lapse between Passover and Pentecost is significant. Pentecost, which began 50 days after the Passover, marked the beginning of the ingathering of the harvest of the nation of Israel. The people went into their fields to gather the fruit and various grains. Pentecost was also called "the feast of weeks" (Exod.

34:22), "the feast of harvest" (Exod. 23:16), and "the day of firstfruits" (Num. 28:26).

According to Leviticus 23:22, the harvest had three parts:

1. The main harvest, which consisted of the majority of the harvest.

2. The corners of each field.

3. The gleanings or what was left over, which God commanded the Israelites to leave for the poor and strangers.

This parallels what Jesus told His disciples in Acts 1:8. He mentioned three parts to the disciples' evangelistic ministry:

1. Jerusalem (the main harvest)

2. Judea and Samaria (the corners of the field)

3. The uttermost parts of the earth (the house of Cornelius, the Gentiles, and the strangers)

At Pentecost, believers received power to gather in their harvest beginning with Jerusalem, then Judea and Samaria, then to the uttermost parts of the earth. This fulfilled Old Testament prophecy concerning Pentecost.

Jesus fulfilled our Passover and lifted judgment from the world (John 1:29; 1 Cor. 5:7). He stayed on earth 40 days and then was taken up into Heaven. The Holy Ghost did not come until after Passover. Jesus, our Passover Lamb, ushered in Pentecost.

Some people have been erroneously taught that they were not saved until they received the Holy Ghost and spoke with other tongues. Jesus never said that. Jesus said, *"the world cannot receive* [the Spirit of truth], *because it seeth him not, neither knoweth him"* (John 14:17).

In the same way that Passover preceded Pentecost, we must first have an experience with Jesus, allowing His blood to cleanse us from sin; then we become candidates for the baptism of the Holy Ghost.

Jesus said the Holy Ghost was dwelling with the disciples, but after Pentecost the Holy Ghost would be in the disciples.

> *For he dwelleth with you, and shall be in you* (John 14:17).

First they had to experience Passover—the blood of Jesus. Then they would experience Pentecost—the power of the Holy Ghost.

A Worthy Candidate for Pentecost

Before He ascended into Heaven, Jesus commanded His disciples to tarry for the promise of the Holy Ghost.

> *Behold, I send the promise of my Father upon*
> *you: but tarry ye in the city of Jerusalem,*
> *until ye be endued with power from on high*
> (Luke 24:49).

They had to wait only because the Holy Ghost was making His debut. Now that He has come, however, those who experience a Passover by accepting Jesus Christ, God's Passover Lamb, can receive the baptism of the Holy Ghost.

Many people have not received the Holy Ghost because they feel unworthy. If your own worthiness were the issue, you wouldn't have anything from God. The Christian life is founded on grace from beginning to end.

God does not see you as you are, but He sees you through the blood of Jesus. When Jesus died on the cross, you died with Him. God reckons you to be dead with Christ. *Reckon* means to figure in something, to write it down, to document it, to take inventory. Although you did not die physically, document your death with Christ because God sees you in Him when He died.

That's why you must have a Passover before you can have a Pentecost. Passover makes you worthy and a fit candidate for Pentecost. Passover applies the blood to the doors of your heart. The two side posts and top lentil of a doorway form a cross, which is a type of our coming through the cross of Jesus.

Gaining proper standing with God always requires the death of a substitute. God shed the blood of an innocent animal and clothed Adam and Eve with its skins after the fall (Gen. 3:21). Each Israelite household in Egypt killed an innocent lamb to mark their doors with its blood (Exod. 12:3-7). Years later it took the blood of a sinless, innocent man to atone for sin.

> *The next day John seeth Jesus coming unto him, and saith, Behold the Lamb of God, which taketh away the sin of the world* (John 1:29).
>
> *But God commendeth his love toward us, in that, while we were yet sinners, Christ died for us. Much more then, being now justified by his blood, we shall be saved from wrath through him* (Romans 5:8-9).

In each of these cases, an individual, a household, and the world could not live up to the standards of a holy God. Only the death of a substitute gave the individual, the household, and the world the standing that God demands.

Every area of your life has been put under the blood of Jesus. He has become your *atonement*, which means a covering, to put away, or to cancel. It also means to reconcile and to make at one with.

God says you are worthy to receive the baptism of the Holy Ghost. Jesus has prayed for you to receive the Comforter. Is it based upon your merit? Of course not. You never have and never will live up to the expectations of a holy God. Jesus, who *"ever liveth to make intercession"* (Heb. 7:25), prays confidently because He died in your stead.

Easier Than You Think

Many have made the baptism of the Holy Ghost and the Spirit-filled life so difficult when actually it is quite simple. Many have taught that if you wait long enough, if you pray hard enough, if you lift your hands, sell out, hold on, or hold out, that you will receive the Holy Ghost. While their intentions may be good, their approach is not scriptural.

We can conclude three things regarding receiving the Holy Ghost:

1. Jesus is praying for you to receive.
2. You must experience a Passover before you can receive.
3. If you have had a Passover, you're a worthy candidate to receive the power of Pentecost.

If you have these three things working for you— the prayers of Jesus, the pleading of the blood in His Passover, and anticipation for the power of Pentecost— you are a worthy candidate.

It Begins with a Desire

> *And I say unto you, Ask, and it shall be given you; seek, and ye shall find; knock, and it shall be opened unto you. For every one that asketh receiveth; and he that seeketh findeth; and to him that knocketh it shall be opened* (Luke 11:9-10).

Jesus began His discourse on receiving the Holy Spirit by using a simple three-letter word—"ask." When you ask for something, it implies that you desire it:

> *Blessed are they which do hunger and thirst after righteousness: for they shall be filled* (Matthew 5:6).

Ask!

Notice two words, hunger and thirst, which imply a desire, a longing, an expectation, a want, or a need. God always keeps His children in some of type of need so He can meet that need. He always wants us dependent on Him.

Being hungry or thirsty implies that you are in need, and it causes you to ask. God is always attentive to the cries of His children.

Jesus simply said, "Ask. I know you are hungry and thirsty. I have what you need. Just ask." Asking implies that you both need and want.

> *The Lord is my shepherd; I shall not want* (Psalm 23:1).
>
> *But my God shall supply all your need according to his riches in glory by Christ Jesus* (Philippians 4:19).

God will not let your needs and wants go unattended, especially when you desire to be more like Him.

We Must Seek What We Ask For

Jesus said that those who seek shall find. Seek means to desire. Jesus wants us to desire the Holy Ghost. Would you ask someone for something and have your head or hand turned the other way? Jesus wants our hearts to be lined up with what our lips are saying.

God rewards those who diligently seek Him (Heb. 11:6). Diligently means to be stretched out for that which you are asking. It means to crave as an expectant mother craves unusual foods. Nothing else satisfies her except the specific combination she asked for.

The Holy Ghost, His power, and the change that He alone can bring in your life must be so precious that you will not accept a counterfeit. Nothing else will suffice. Is your heart focused with a desire that will not take "no" for an answer? Do you really want the power of the Holy Ghost? Jesus taught the Parable of the Lost Coin:

> *Either what woman having ten pieces of silver, if she lose one piece, doth not light a candle, and sweep the house, and seek diligently till she find it? And when she hath found it, she calleth her friends and her neighbours together, saying, Rejoice with me; for I have found the piece which I had lost* (Luke 15:8-9).

When this woman realized she didn't have her precious coin, she lit a candle, swept the house, and searched diligently until she found it. We must be in the same place of earnest seeking in regard to the Holy Ghost.

Upon realizing we don't have the fullness of the Holy Ghost, we light a candle. The psalmist wrote:

> *The entrance of thy words giveth light* (Psalm 119:130).

We must sweep our house, which means we purge ourselves of anything that isn't of God. Then we must seek the Holy Ghost diligently.

We must earnestly want the Holy Ghost and refuse to compromise. You can be real and have the Holy Ghost. It isn't something mysterious. This is God's will for your life!

You Have to Knock!

Those who want the power of the Holy Ghost must take a three-step approach: ask, seek, and knock. What prompts you to open your front door? When someone knocks, you see who it is and what they want.

Jesus said to knock.

Before knocking, you must have a desire to ask. This driving desire caused you to come to the door with great expectation and determination. You searched until you found the door and now you knock.

It may seem that Jesus has these steps out of order, but that's not true. If you have no will to ask, there's no reason to knock. Without the will to seek, there's no reason to knock. Knocking is preceded by a will to ask and search diligently. Knocking gives you access to what you have diligently sought.

How Much More...

An earthly father can be very biased. Sometimes he is stubborn, and sometimes he gives for all the wrong reasons. Jesus made it very clear: If the child asks for one thing, the Father will not give another. He then asked a question:

> *If ye then, being evil, know how to give good*
> *gifts unto your children: how much more shall*
> *your heavenly Father give the Holy Spirit to*

them that ask him? (Luke 11:13) The emphasis is on "how much more."

God knows that we need the power of the Holy Ghost.
Spiritual gifts function only as the Holy Ghost empowers the child of God. As you ask and seek, remember
that God knows your motives. He endues you with the
power of the Holy Ghost to give you victory over satan,
to make you joyful, and to enable you to function in the
gifts of the Spirit.

God wants you to have the power of the Holy Ghost.
He gives us a simple, three-step approach: ask, seek,
and knock. Take the Word as authoritative. Be like the
woman who had lost her precious coin. She wanted it
so badly that she searched with a candle and swept her
house clean.

The Power of the Holy Ghost

Old Testament types have their fulfillment in the New
Testament. Daniel wrote about a fourth man in the fiery
furnace with the three Hebrew children; Moses spoke
of the rock that followed the children of Israel; each
Israelite household killed a lamb for their Passover. All
of these were types of Christ.

The Holy Ghost is likened to wind or breath.

> *The wind bloweth where it listeth, and thou*
> *hearest the sound thereof, but canst not tell*

> *whence it cometh, and whither it goeth: so is every one that is born of the Spirit* (John 3:8).
>
> *And suddenly there came a sound from heaven as of a rushing mighty wind, and it filled all the house where they were sitting* (Acts 2:2).

The power of the Holy Ghost can make you everything God said you could be. Adam illustrates this perfectly. The Bible says that Adam was only a form until God breathed on him (Gen. 2:7). Only then did Adam become a living soul.

Until then he had potential but no power. When God breathed into Adam, he received the power to reach his potential. The mere form of man became a living soul. The word *living* means to be vibrant, alive, and strong.

You have great potential in your life. With great potential comes great responsibility. God has shaped you, but you need power to become everything He desires for you to become. Without the power of the Holy Ghost you can go to Heaven, but you will never reach your potential. Your ministry, your gifts, your calling, your life, and your marriage will be only a form of what it could have been.

> *Without the Holy Ghost, you will never reach your full potential.*

An Exceedingly Great Army

Without a word from God, without the energizing breath of the Holy Ghost, you are only a mere form of what you can be. This is similar to the valley of dry bones that Ezekiel saw. Before the prophet lay a potential army, but without the Word of the Lord they were merely a form of what they could have been.

Let's look at some principles we can learn from Ezekiel 37:

1. You must be willing to confess your condition. "They were very dry" (vs. 2).

2. You must confess that you are merely a form of what you could be.

    ■ The valley was "full of bones" (vs. 1).

    ■ The structure of an army was just waiting for God's command.

3. You must hear the Word of God. "Prophesy upon these dry bones, and say unto them, O ye dry bones, hear the word of the Lord" (vs. 4).

    ■ The anointing only falls upon truth. God will not put His seal of approval on something until He is sure that it is His.

- The Word brings the truth that ultimately sets us free (John 8:32).

4. The Word will bring about change.

- The dry bones heard and were quickened (vs. 4).

- They heard their potential. "I will cause breath to enter into you, and ye shall live" (vs. 5).

- They knew they were not complete at this stage. "I will lay sinews upon you, and will bring flesh upon you, and cover you with skin" (vs. 6). The Word brought about a noise as broken pieces began to come together (vs. 7). God will speak to your broken and shattered dreams.

- The Word brought a shaking (vs. 7). We need to be shaken out of our complacency, tradition, formalism, and doctrines.

- The Word formed real people with arms, legs, eyes, and feet. They were still not complete, however. "But there was no breath in them" (vs. 8).

5. The potential was realized as the word brought about the wind. "Prophesy unto the wind, prophesy, son of man, and say to the wind, Thus saith the Lord God; Come from the four winds, O breath, and breathe upon these slain, that they may live" (vs. 9).

The wind gave potential, the ability to carry out what they were capable of doing. The Word came from the four corners of the earth. That tells me there isn't an area that God cannot fill with the Holy Ghost. Your past, your childhood, your feelings of inferiority, your wounds, your loneliness. The Holy Ghost can fill you from the north, south, east, and west.

This pile of bones had a potential that Ezekiel couldn't see just as you have unseen potential. No matter what others say, God sees incredible potential in you. The Word of God says you're capable. Within you is an army. You merely need the wind to breathe upon that which God has formed in you.

Within you is an army.

Thoughts and Reflections

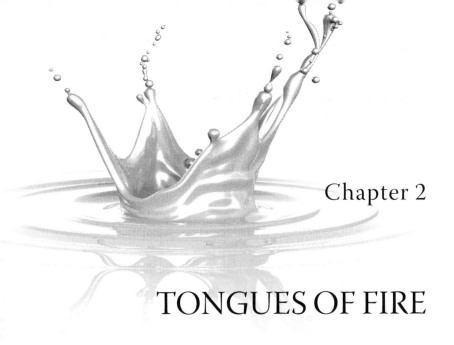

Chapter 2

TONGUES OF FIRE

Before the day of Pentecost, the Holy Ghost had come upon men and women periodically, usually to empower them for specific tasks given by God as portrayed in the Old Testament. Pentecost fulfilled Old Testament prophecy and many predictions made by Jesus Himself.

Christ taught His disciples to pray, "*Thy kingdom come*" (Matt. 6:10). The apostle Paul said, "*The kingdom of God is not meat and drink* [it was not by observing any particular feast, custom, or ritual]; *but righteousness, and peace, and joy in the Holy Ghost*" (Rom. 14:17).

The Holy Ghost came as the authority and power of the Kingdom of God. The disciples had witnessed the miracles of Jesus. They saw His death and burial.

They also saw the resurrected Christ stand in their presence three days later, which amazed them. Even Thomas, who was a doubter, stood in awe and declared, *"My Lord and my God"* (John 20:28)! Even though they had seen and testified to this, the disciples could not just go on their way preaching. Jesus had given them specific instructions:

> *Tarry ye in the city of Jerusalem, until ye be endued with power from on high* (Luke 24:49).

God wanted a witness from Heaven to empower mankind.

Only an earthen vessel empowered from Heaven could declare the glories of the world to come (Rom. 9:23).

The doctrine of speaking in tongues and being baptized in the Holy Ghost has been accompanied by much controversy. Let's turn to the Scriptures to look at the initial outpouring of the Holy Ghost.

> *And when the day of Pentecost was fully come, they were all with one accord in one place. And suddenly there came a sound from heaven as of a rushing mighty wind, and it filled all the house where they were sitting. And there appeared unto them cloven tongues like as of fire, and it sat upon each of them. And they were all filled with the*

Holy Ghost, and began to speak with other tongues, as the Spirit gave them utterance (Acts 2:1-4).

What happened on the day of Pentecost?

1. This event came right on time. "And when the day of Pentecost was fully come" (vs. 1).

2. A sound from Heaven, like a rushing mighty wind, filled all the house where they were sitting (vs. 2).

3. Tongues of fire "sat upon each of them" (vs. 3).

4. They "were all filled with the Holy Ghost, and began to speak with other tongues" (vs. 4).

5. The language came "as the Spirit gave them utterance" (vs. 4b).

Pentecost Had Fully Come

The Jewish people were familiar with the term Pentecost. Everything God did in types and shadows in the Old Testament was fulfilled in the New Testament. In the Old Testament God revealed Himself in many ways to Israel. He was known as the "I am," promising to sustain them on their journey from Egypt to Canaan.

Whatever they needed, He was the I am of sustenance for that very thing.

One word gives us an understanding of this concept—the word *true*. Jesus said:

> *My Father giveth you the true bread from*
> *heaven* (John 6:32).

True means "to have without concealment." Throughout the Old Testament, God had been concealed in type and shadow. In the New Testament, however, He is no longer concealed. He became in reality everything that He merely was a shadow of in the Old Testament.

Pentecost was a type of something that one day would explode and change this world for eternity. *Pentecost* meant "fiftieth day." When we read "the day of Pentecost had fully come," that means the fiftieth day after Passover had arrived.

Everything that needed to precede this memorable day had taken place. Jesus, the Passover Lamb, had died and risen from the dead. He had walked with His disciples, was confirmed for 40 days and nights with many infallible proofs, and then was received into glory.

Our personal Passover must precede our Pentecost. The blood of Christ prepares us for Pentecost, washing away our sin and prejudice, enabling us to come together with devout men and women from every nation. You cannot have a Pentecost with God if you are biased against people—not just racial prejudice but experiential prejudice. People have devised a grading scale between one and ten for the severity of certain sins. Sin, which simply means to miss the mark, has no scale of severity in the eyes of God.

God is tearing down racial, ethnic, and religious barriers, bringing people together from all walks of life in one place with one focus: to reach the world for Jesus. We need it to be said of us, "The day of Pentecost has fully come." The word *fully* means to come with an expected end, to come with anticipation, to come to have a part in a mission.

> *God is bringing people together to reach the world for Jesus.*

Pentecost marked the beginning of a mission for the Jewish people as they gathered in the fruit of their labors. Pentecost in Acts 2 marked the beginning of a mission for the church to gather in lost souls. We need Pentecost to fully arise in our life as we fall in love with Jesus, the Passover Lamb, to carry out the ingathering of His harvest.

The Sound Filled the House

The sound from Heaven "filled all the house where they were sitting." This sound was a sign, witnessing that Heaven was speaking. The Greek word for sound denotes a loud rumbling or roaring voice, much like the rumbling of a tornado that precedes the storm.

This wind filled closets, bedrooms, bathrooms, upstairs, and downstairs. It filled all the components in the house: jars, glasses, significant and insignificant things. This indicates that anyone can be filled with the Holy Ghost.

We have seen saved Baptists, Methodists, Catholics—all walks of Christian professions—filled with the Holy Ghost with the evidence of speaking with other tongues. The only mandatory prerequisite is that you be a believer—a born again, blood-washed child of God (Acts 2:38-39; John 14:17).

What about the place where you are sitting? What about your home church? Is it filled with the Holy Ghost? Has your assembly experienced a Pentecost that is filling everything inside? A person becomes a product of his environment. You will begin to resemble whatever you are around, whether it is good or bad.

Tongues of Fire Sat on Each One

This experience was not for a select few. The cloven tongues of fire rested upon each one—men and women, young and old, apostles and disciples. Hearing the sound, the amazed multitude asked, "What do these things mean?" Apostle Peter stood and said:

*This is that which was spoken by the prophet
Joel; and it shall come to pass in the last days,
saith God, I will pour out of my Spirit upon
all flesh: and your sons and your daughters
shall prophesy, and your young men shall see
visions, and your old men shall dream dreams:
and on my servants and on my handmaidens
I will pour out in those days of my Spirit; and
they shall prophesy* (Acts 2:16-18).

God planned for His Spirit, a consuming fire, to rest upon each of His children. Apostle Peter told the crowd:

*For the promise is unto you, and to your chil-
dren, and to all that are afar off, even as many
as the Lord our God shall call* (Acts 2:39).

Peter, who later preached to the Gentiles in Cornelius's house, said:

*Of a truth I perceive that God is no respecter
of persons* (Acts 10:34).

He saw the Holy Spirit fall on the assembly even before he finished his sermon, confirming God's promise.

They Spoke with Other Tongues

They "*began to speak with other tongues*" (Acts 2:4). *Tongues* in this passage is the Greek word *glossa*, which simply means "a language."

Devout Jews from every nation had gathered in Jerusalem for Pentecost. When the Holy Spirit was poured out and the disciples began to speak in tongues, it caused quite a stir.

> *Now when this was noised abroad, the multitude came together, and were confounded, because that every man heard them speak in his own language. And they were all amazed and marvelled, saying one to another, Behold, are not all these which speak Galilaeans? And how hear we every man in our own tongue, wherein we were born? Parthians, and Medes, and Elamites, and the dwellers in Mesopotamia, and in Judaea, and Cappadocia, in Pontus, and Asia, Phrygia, and Pamphylia, in Egypt, and in the parts of Libya about Cyrene, and strangers of Rome, Jews and proselytes, Cretes and Arabians, we do hear them speak in our tongues the wonderful works of God* (Acts 2:6-11).

Luke mentions over a dozen locations in this passage, representing many languages and dialects. Tongues enabled the multitude to hear the mighty deeds of God in their own language.

The Spirit Gave Them Utterance

The language came *"as the Spirit gave them utterance"* (Acts 2:4). *Utterance* means the ability to speak plainly, to declare openly, or to have the ability to enunciate with clarity. The people spoke, but the words came through the ability or enabling of the Holy Ghost. They spoke as the Spirit gave utterance.

When you do something you are doing it with assistance. If you walk across the room, you are walking as your feet move. Your feet are the tool being used to carry out the mission of walking.

Suppose you fly to Chicago. It could be said that you traveled to Chicago as the plane flew, meaning that you flew by the auspice of the plane.

The believers at Pentecost spoke the language of Heaven, but only as the Holy Ghost gave them utterance.

God Gave a Pattern

The Old Testament conveyed many truths, but they were concealed in types and shadows. Everything in the Old Testament tabernacle depicted in some type or shadow the glory of God in the face of Jesus Christ.

The tabernacle was not an idea imagined by Moses. As God gave him the blueprint, Moses built it after the pattern he saw in Heaven (Exod. 25:8-40).

*Moses was admonished of God when he
was about to make the tabernacle: for, See,
saith he, that thou make all things according
to the pattern shewed to thee in the mount*
(Hebrews 8:5).

Moses merely built what Heaven had envisioned.
Tongues are no different than a pattern.

As Moses was commanded to build by the pattern,
so we are to speak by the pattern as the Spirit gives
utterance. Tongues come because the Spirit gives the
utterance or the ability to speak or enunciate.

People with hearing problems almost always have
a speech impediment. Our ability to hear gives us the
ability to articulate or enunciate. Without hearing, we
are limited in our ability to speak. The same is true in
the Spirit.

We must hear before we can speak. At Pentecost
they heard *"a sound from heaven as of a rushing mighty
wind. ...And they...began to speak with other tongues, as
the Spirit gave them utterance"* (Acts 2:2,4). They heard
the sound, then they spoke.

God said Israel would not hear Him because of
their uncircumcised ears. This simply means they were
carnal and fleshly. We must walk in the Spirit to hear the
Spirit. To understand the ways of God, we must listen
not to human logic but to the One who *"knoweth what
is the mind of the Spirit"* (Rom. 8:27).

In the Old Testament, God spoke a pattern of what He wanted to be built on earth. God also used a sound to witness to the Old Testament saints. God hasn't changed His methods for we who live today.

Exodus 28:33-35 describes the design of the high priest's garment. On the hem of his garment were pomegranates of blue, purple, and scarlet, symbolizing freshness of life, royalty, and the blood.

A golden bell was fastened on either side of the fruit for a sign to the people. When the high priest went into the holy place to minister as mediator, he took blood and offered it upon the mercy seat. The people could not see him, but if they heard the golden bells they knew the sacrifice had been accepted and the priest lived. This sound was a sign for the people that their sins had been atoned for.

After the resurrection of Christ, He showed Himself to the disciples and others for 40 days. Before ascending to Heaven, Jesus told His followers to wait for the promise of the Father. They gathered for prayer and waited as Christ took up the office of high priest forever.

The Jews knew that the Passover resulted in the death of an innocent lamb. Fifty days later marked the beginning of their harvest or the feast of ingathering. Jesus said He was the Passover Lamb. Pentecost marked 50 days since His blood had been poured out for the forgiveness of sins.

The disciples' wait ended. *"And when the day of Pentecost was fully come...there came a sound"* (Acts 2:1-2). This was the fulfillment of the pomegranates and golden bells. The bells were a sign that the sacrifice had been accepted, and the Holy Ghost was the sound that our sins had been atoned for.

Have Tongues Ceased?

> *Charity never faileth: but whether there be prophecies, they shall fail; whether there be tongues, they shall cease; whether there be knowledge, it shall vanish away. For we know in part, and we prophesy in part. But when that which is perfect is come, then that which is in part shall be done away* (1 Corinthians 13:8-10).

Many denominations have interpreted this verse to mean that spiritual gifts, including tongues, have ceased. But is this theory accurate?

They say "that which is perfect" is the complete, written Scriptures. If this is the case, then knowledge is also done away with—and we know that isn't true. By putting the verse in context, tongues, prophecies, and knowledge still exist because "that which is perfect" (the second coming of Christ) has not yet taken place.

The gifts of the Spirit enable us to see a glimpse of His glory, but we still *"know in part, and we prophesy in part"* (1 Cor. 13:9). The shadow, the images, the glimpse of His glory will pale in comparison to Christ Himself when He reigns in glory. The gifts help us and attend to many of our needs. But when we see Jesus face to face, we will graduate from gifts, which are only a glimpse, to the giver—Jesus Christ Himself.

No matter how spiritual we become, no matter how much Greek and Hebrew we may learn, and no matter how much we pray and study, our understanding of God at its best is only partial.

> *For now we see through a glass, darkly; but then face to face: now I know in part; but then shall I know even as also I am known* (1 Corinthians 13:12).

Until then, however, tongues continue for the use and edification of the believer.

Why Tongues?

God chose tongues as a sign for a significant reason. We can understand His sovereign selection of tongues from this passage:

> *For in many things we offend all. If any man offend not in word, the same is a perfect man, and able also to bridle the whole body.*

Behold, we put bits in the horses' mouths, that they may obey us; and we turn about their whole body. Behold also the ships, which though they be so great, and are driven of fierce winds, yet are they turned about with a very small helm, whithersoever the governor listeth. Even so the tongue is a little member, and boasteth great things. Behold, how great a matter a little fire kindleth!

And the tongue is a fire, a world of iniquity: so is the tongue among our members, that it defileth the whole body, and setteth on fire the course of nature; and it is set on fire of hell. For every kind of beasts, and of birds, and of serpents, and of things in the sea, is tamed, and hath been tamed of mankind: but the tongue can no man tame; it is an unruly evil, full of deadly poison (James 3:2-8).

Let's summarize some of these truths:

1. Every beast and animal has been tamed by mankind except the tongue.

2. If we can control the tongue, we can control the whole body.

3. Very large things can be controlled by something very small.

4. The tongue is a fire.

God often employs natural examples to bring about spiritual understanding. Jesus often used natural, physical, tangible analogies in His parables. He talked about a man who sowed seed, a woman who searched for a lost coin, and servants who invested their master's money to describe the Kingdom of God.

In this passage God uses the tongue to teach truth. The tongue is a fire—something out of control, something that is difficult if not impossible to tame. If we can control the tongue, this enables us to control every aspect of our lives.

> *Taming the tongue gives us power to control our lives.*

James pointed out that something very large can be guided by something very small. A horse can be controlled by the bits in its mouth. James knew a horse wasn't tamed by chaining its feet or wrapping something around its neck. A horse can be guided by controlling its movements from the mouth.

A large ship can be guided across rough waters with little effort by using a small wheel, the helm, which guides the ship and controls its direction.

When we are filled with the Holy Ghost, He acts as a deterrent. He places bits in our mouths and bridles our speech. Just when you feel like telling someone off, the Holy Ghost takes control. Isn't it exciting that God took the tongue, a member of our body known for being "a fire, a world of iniquity," and sanctified it for His purposes?

When God filled the disciples on the day of Pentecost, He sent tongues of fire to sit upon each of them. God caused them to speak with a heavenly language, proving He had control of these believers.

Why did God choose tongues as a sign? He took the most difficult, uncontrollable member of our body and caused it to yield to divinely inspired speech. Bridling the tongue may be impossible for man to do in his own strength, but the supernatural outpouring of the Holy Ghost enabled these disciples to use their tongues for the purposes of God.

Two Types of Tongues

Speaking in tongues can occur in two different settings. A believer may pray in tongues privately to commune with God:

> *For he that speaketh in an unknown tongue speaketh not unto men, but unto God: for no man understandeth him; howbeit in the spirit he speaketh mysteries. ...He that speaketh in an unknown tongue edifieth himself* (1 Corinthians 14:2,4).

Scripture also teaches on the gift of tongues or "divers [different] kinds of tongues" (1 Cor. 12:10), which are used in a public assembly. The apostle Paul gave instructions on regulating this gift.

> *If any man speak in an unknown tongue, let it be by two, or at the most by three, and that by course; and let one interpret* (1 Corinthians 14:27).

Without the interpretation of tongues, the church will not be edified.

> *I would that ye all spake with tongues but rather that ye prophesied: for greater is he that prophesieth than he that speaketh with tongues, except he interpret, that the church may receive edifying* (1 Corinthians 14:5).

We also find the phrase "to one is given" (1 Cor. 12:8), which implies that not all will have the same gift any more than members of a body have the same functions. A body has many members, yet their functions differ from each other. The hand cannot function as a foot or vice versa. In the same way the Spirit gives different gifts to different people. We also find in 1 Corinthians 12:4-7 four important truths:

1. Gifts come by the Spirit (vs. 4).

2. Each gift has a different administration (vs. 5).

3. Each gift has a different operation (vs. 6).

4. Gifts are given "to every man to profit withal" (vs. 7).

The gifts of the Spirit are always manifested to minister and help people, never to cause harm, confusion, or division.

There is a difference between the gift of tongues and tongues used as a prayer language. The gift of tongues benefits the hearers; the prayer language benefits only the speaker. If you fail to understand the difference between speaking in tongues and the gift of tongues, you have missed the whole issue and will become confused. As a result, you may even confuse others.

> *The gift of tongues benefits hearers; the prayer language benefits the speaker.*

When the gift of tongues is given in a public assembly, the message needs to be interpreted for the hearers to benefit. Sometimes, however, such as on the day of Pentecost, the gift of tongues is given to minister to the hearers in their own language (Acts 2:6).

For example, suppose you were in Russia and the Holy Spirit enabled you to speak fluent Russian. This miraculous sign would cause the people to understand in their own language and it would be a witness and a confirmation of the gift itself.

> *In the law it is written, With men of other tongues and other lips will I speak unto this people; and yet for all that will they not hear me, saith the Lord. Wherefore tongues are for a sign, not to them that believe, but to them that believe not: but prophesying serveth not for them that believe not, but for them which believe* (1 Corinthians 14:21-22).

God said that He would speak to men in other tongues and with other lips, "yet for all that will they not hear me." Isn't it amazing that men can see the gift of God in operation and hear the manifestation of the Holy Ghost but fail to believe? Mockers concluded, "These men are full of new wine" (Acts 2:13).

Being filled with the Holy Ghost, however, gives us tremendous power for living the Christian life.

Empowerment Not Entertainment

The Holy Ghost has not been given to the church to entertain congregations but rather to empower them. Jesus said, "*Ye shall receive power, after that the Holy*

Ghost is come upon you" (Acts 1:8). The Holy Ghost gives us power not to just shout, run the aisles, or to put on a show. He empowers us to intervene in society as a witness.

Jesus gave these instructions to His disciples:

> *And these signs shall follow them that believe; In my name shall they cast out devils; they shall speak with new tongues; they shall take up serpents; and if they drink any deadly thing, it shall not hurt them; they shall lay hands on the sick, and they shall recover* (Mark 16:17-18).

The Book of Acts records the amazing signs and wonders that occurred through the disciples. What was the catalyst for these miracles? Pentecost. After being endued with power from on high, *"they went forth, and preached every where, the Lord working with them, and confirming the word with signs following"* (Mark 16:20).

That's the kind of power we need to transform our lives, families, churches, and society.

Thoughts and Reflections

_____

_____

_____

CHAPTER 3

POWER FOR LIVING

Being filled with the Holy Ghost places the power of God at our disposal to carry out the work of the Kingdom. Soon after being baptized in the Holy Ghost, most believers notice a marked change in their ability to pray and walk in God's anointing.

Why is it so important to pray with the power of the Holy Ghost? All too often our spirit is willing, but our flesh is weak. We need God's help to overcome the tug of our carnal nature.

Our spirit is willing but our flesh is weak.

Man Is Body, Soul, and Spirit

The apostle Paul wrote:

> *And I pray God your whole spirit and soul and body be preserved blameless unto the coming of our Lord Jesus Christ* (1 Thessalonians 5:23).

This Scripture shows us the three parts of man: body, soul, and spirit.

If these three parts were the same, Paul never would have prayed that they each would be wholly preserved. If we want to have a successful prayer life and reach our full potential with God, then each of these parts must be understood and put in their place.

Each of these parts affects our prayer life. If we were only spirit, the blessings of prayer would be unrestrained, without hindrance. But we have to deal with our body and soul.

The words *wholly* and *preserved* are significant. *Wholly* means to completely, absolutely reach the limit or potential. *Preserved* means to guard, to watch, to keep an eye on, to keep something in its place. As we pray, we must contend with these three parts. Each element plays a significant role in the success or failure of our prayer life.

1. Body

The body entails our flesh and its appetites. The flesh never wants to pray. The flesh never awakens you with a desire to seek God. The flesh is at enmity with

God and does not understand His ways. This is why no man can please God in the flesh. Because the flesh will never come up to the expectations of the Spirit, we must discipline the flesh to be subject to what we know is right. The flesh will sit back and say, "You don't have to pray. If it's going to happen, then it will happen." But we must go into combat to get certain things. We must bombard the gates of Heaven to obtain certain things, and the body never wants to do this.

2. Soul

The soul of man is sandwiched between our body, which never wants to pray or do right, and our spirit, which desires God and spiritual things. The soul of man entails our emotions, feelings, weaknesses, and our past. An ongoing, progressive, renewing work occurs in your soul. When we pray with our soul, we pray with our intellect and an understanding to the best of our ability. But to go into deep spiritual warfare, we must go beyond our logic and our intellect.

3. Spirit

When you were lost, your spirit was *"dead in trespasses and sins"* (Eph. 2:1). Now that you are saved, however, your spirit has been quickened, which means to vitalize, to cause to live, to be vibrant and strong. As the Holy Ghost begins to have an intimate relationship with our spirit, we begin to produce the *"fruit of the Spirit"* (Gal. 5:22-23). The Holy Ghost wants to know you in an intimate way; He doesn't want just a surface relationship.

> *Adam knew his wife again; and she bare a son, and called his name Seth* (Genesis 4:25).

Intimacy results in fruit or offspring. The apostle Paul wrote, *"that I may know Him"* (Phil. 3:10), which implies a close relationship, one that causes us to partake in His experiences. But you can't know Christ in resurrection power until you know Him in His sufferings and death. Our old man must be crucified with Him daily as we are being changed from glory to glory.

The apostle Paul knew Jesus in the pardon and forgiveness of sin, but still longed to know Him intimately. For this to occur, two things had to happen.

- *"Forgetting those things which are behind"* (Phil. 3:13). These were not all bad or questionable activities, but they were not satisfying either. They left Paul crying out for more of God.

- *"Reaching forth unto those things which are before"* (Phil. 3:13). Paul wanted to press toward the mark for the prize of the high calling of God in Christ Jesus. He wanted to become spiritually intimate with Jesus to produce fruit.

Why Speak in Tongues?

This is a good question asked by many intelligent people. Why should anyone speak in tongues? Tongues merely express the language of God. In order for us to reach the will of God for our lives, we must be able to communicate with God.

We must communicate with God.

Speaking in tongues is not a strange new doctrine. In fact, it's been around for hundreds, even thousands, of years. God poured it out at the inception of the Church.

Before we cover several scriptural reasons for this practice, I would like to share an example that highlights the importance of speaking in tongues.

A CB radio gives you the ability to speak to other people providing you are on the same frequency. Different people use different channels for a variety of reasons. Whatever channel you use to transmit or receive a message, the transmitter and the one receiving must be on the same channel and have the squelch turned up loud enough to hear. CB radios also have a special channel for emergencies. Any time you need the police or emergency assistance you can switch to this frequency and no one else can monitor your conversation.

This may seem like a crude analogy, but in the spirit world many messages are being transmitted. The Bible says that satan is the *"prince of the power of the air"* (Eph. 2:2). If we stay on the same frequency, he can pick up our transmissions. But satan cannot monitor the emergency channel. His squelch cannot tune in because it is just a bunch of static to him. He cannot make out what we are saying.

Praying in the Spirit is a frequency that satan cannot pick up.

Bypassing Satan's Radar

And I heard a loud voice saying in heaven, Now is come salvation, and strength, and the kingdom of our God, and the power of his Christ: for the accuser of our brethren is cast down, which accused them before our God day and night (Revelation 12:10).

Since satan is the prince of the power of the air and comes before the presence of God, he constantly surveys our prayer life. No wonder we experience such adversity and opposition when we try to get close to God. To make our way to the throne of God, we must push past the enemy's surveillance.

For we wrestle not against flesh and blood, but against principalities, against powers, against the rulers of the darkness of this world, against spiritual wickedness in high places (Ephesians 6:12).

Let me use another illustration. In the first Iraq War, the United States and their allies knew that they were up against some of the most modern, up-to-date defenses in all the world.

The war was waged in two parts. During the first part, known as Desert Watch or Desert Shield, the United States flew reconnaissance flights to monitor the movement and the strengths and weaknesses of the enemy.

Because of these reconnaissance flights, we learned that Iraq had employed the most modern, state-of-the-art radar systems. The United States knew if we were to be successful—with limited casualties—we would have to somehow bypass Iraq's radar system. This was achieved by using stealth bombers, which enabled us to mount an attack without being detected on radar.

On the first night of the attack, the major bombardment was almost over before Iraq even realized what had happened.

When you pray in the Spirit, you go before the throne of God undetected by satan because you speak mysteries to Him. Your prayers are like stealth bombers that bypass his detection.

> ### *Your prayers are like stealth bombers bypassing satan.*

Praying in the Spirit enables you to pray healing, delivering, yoke-breaking, devil-stomping prayers without being shot at. You can go into God's presence and receive ammunition to shake the gates of hell. That's why satan fights to keep people from praying in the Spirit. He confuses people regarding this truth because he knows he doesn't have a weapon to defend against it.

Switch Channels

The apostle Paul uses the word *tongues* (plural) to show his multiplicity of languages. *"Though I speak with the tongues of men and of angels"* (1 Cor. 13:1).

Sometimes we need to speak in our natural language according to our heritage. Sometimes, however, our natural language is no match for the warring spirits between earth and the throne of God.

When prayers in our natural language are being intercepted and shot down, Paul tells us to switch channels. Allow the Holy Ghost within you to speak out on earth what Heaven is speaking into your spirit. This is praying in tongues, or praying in the Spirit.

Satan understands the language of men. When we pray about a certain thing, our adversary causes principalities and powers in the atmosphere between earth and the throne of God to intercept our words. He attacks the very thing we pray about.

Satan does not understand the language of Heaven. God's ways, which are so much higher than our ways, include praying in tongues. This leaves satan confused as to how to attack us. He may assign an evil spirit to attack our prayer life and report back to him so he can make a counterattack. But when we pray in the Spirit, or pray in tongues, we frustrate his plans.

Remember that tongues are spiritual and not fleshly. Satan works through our flesh. When our prayers switch from an earthly, fleshly, carnal language to a secondary, spiritual, heavenly language, satan is confused.

The believer is built up as the Holy Ghost pleads the life, the power, the joy, and the victory of God into your spirit. Hallelujah for the ability to speak out from earth what the Holy Ghost is speaking in from Heaven!

Interceding with Groans

Speaking in tongues places a great arsenal of spiritual weaponry at your disposal. Not knowing this, however, many believers struggle in prayer and intercession.

> *Likewise the Spirit also helpeth our infirmities: for we know not what we should pray for as we ought: but the Spirit itself maketh intercession for us with groanings which cannot*

be uttered. And he that searcheth the hearts knoweth what is the mind of the Spirit, because he maketh intercession for the saints according to the will of God (Romans 8:26-27).

Romans 8:26 contains a word that is often overlooked, and that is the very first word, likewise. The word means "in like manner, or to be similar to."

For we know that the whole creation groaneth and travaileth in pain together until now. And not only they, but ourselves also, which have the firstfruits of the Spirit, even we ourselves groan within ourselves, waiting for the adoption, to wit, the redemption of our body (Romans 8:22-23).

It points back to the two previous times the word groan is used in that chapter. Romans 8:22 refers to the groan of creation waiting for the redemption and restoration of this earth. Romans 8:23 refers to the groans of Christians as we await the completion of our redemption, the receiving of our new body.

The apostle Paul uses the same word for the groans of the Holy Ghost (Rom. 8:26). The word *groanings* means "to groan with a sigh, or a sense of lamenting."

This was very familiar to the Old Testament prophets. When they got in tune with the nature and character of God, they often expressed themselves in unusual ways. Their intercession for the people could be described as wailing, howling, or lamenting. They were speaking a language outwardly that God was speaking inwardly to them.

We cannot understand the language of God in our own intellect.

> *We cannot understand the language of God in our own intellect.*

I like to explain it like this: When a child who cannot talk plainly wants something, he or she may be able to speak only portions of words. A stranger may not understand, but the child's mother can make out the language. Even though the baby talk is barely intelligible, she understands the need. Taking a bunch of stammering, broken remarks, she interprets the language to meet the need.

Sometimes in order to get what you need from God, you must go from one language (our human intellect) to another language (the Holy Ghost).

Help in Prayer

The Holy Ghost stands alongside us to assist, to cause one to stand, to cause one to achieve. It means one who stands in covenant with. In essence, the Holy Ghost stands by your side to not only plead the covenant of God, but to cause you to attain what the covenant provides for you.

He does this in four ways:

1. *He assists us through our infirmities.*

The Spirit "helpeth our infirmities" which means He stands alongside as an ally, one waiting in the wings who is willing and able to assist us. We need help because *"the spirit indeed is willing, but the flesh is weak"* (Matt. 26:41).

The word *infirmities* means inability to produce results. Opposition prevents you from receiving what God has provided for you in His covenant. The Holy Ghost helps us and gives us a breakthrough.

2. *He assists us in that He knows.*

The Spirit is very knowledgeable about things that perplex us. "For we know not what we should pray for." We don't always know what is right. As we allow the Holy Ghost to saturate and to permeate our lives, He begins to tell us how to pray for certain things.

For instance, whom should you date? Whom should you marry? Where should you go to church? In what ministry should you serve? Sometimes you'll want to speak or do something and the Holy Ghost will caution you, "Don't say or do that." He assists you where you don't have clear direction.

3. He assists us with intercessions.

As Jesus, our Mediator, pleads us to God, the Holy Ghost, who knows the very mind of God, pleads God to us. "He maketh intercession for us." Intercession means that the Holy Ghost will meet with us. He comes into our situation and speaks into our spirit as one who interviews another.

We don't have the ability to produce results and to get our breakthrough. Even if we did have the ability, we are still void of knowledge because we "know not what we should pray for." The Holy Ghost will get us to admit our frailties. Then He will fellowship with us and assist us in what to do. As the Holy Ghost intercedes, He merely speaks into earth what He has already heard spoken in the counsels of Heaven.

This is why Jesus often repeated a truth He wanted to reveal: "Verily, verily" or "truly, truly."

Once in the heavenlies by divine sanction, once in the earth to carry out the divine sanction.

4. He assists us with Heaven's language.

The Spirit pleads the will of God to us. *"Because he maketh intercession for the saints according to the will of God"* (Rom. 8:27). As creation groans, it speaks a language that only God can interpret. The saints of God sometimes groan with broken, stammering remarks.

Sometimes all we can do is lay before God, not knowing what to do or say. We need to be full of the

Holy Ghost and listening to Him because He will plead God's will to us. We just have to be able to hear. *"He that hath an ear, let him hear what the Spirit saith unto the churches"* (Rev. 2:7).

> ## *The Holy Ghost pleads God's will to us.*

The Holy Ghost Relays What Heaven Sends

John 16:13 presents some of the greatest truths ever revealed to the Church. Jesus said the Holy Ghost would do four things:

1. He will guide you into all truth.
2. He will speak truth to you, but He will not speak of Himself.
3. He will show you all truth concerning things to come.
4. He will speak into you what He hears Heaven speaking into Him.

We must be able to hear what the Holy Ghost is saying. But it is equally important to know the Holy Ghost hears what to speak to us. He never breaks the chain of command from Heaven. How can we know that what the Holy Ghost says is reliable?

First, the Holy Ghost is one with God. He will never speak anything that is not sanctioned by the Word. Second, God, who cannot lie, searched Heaven and earth for someone to confirm His covenant and swear to its authenticity. When He could find no one else to meet the criteria of His holy demands, God swore by Himself. Now the Holy Ghost freely speaks a sworn oath and covenant into the hearts of Spirit-filled believers who can hear His voice.

Jesus said, "whatsoever he heareth, he speaketh." That means the Holy Ghost speaks into you what Heaven has already decreed.

Build Up Yourself

In the following passage we find some of the simplest and most profound truths in all the Word of God. But everything hinges on the truth stated in verse 20:

> *But ye, beloved, building up yourselves on your most holy faith, praying in the Holy Ghost, keep yourselves in the love of God, looking for the mercy of our Lord Jesus Christ unto eternal life. And of some have compassion, making a difference: and others save with fear, pulling them out of the fire; hating even the garment spotted by the flesh* (Jude 20-23).

We can build up ourselves, cultivate a sense of expectancy about the coming of the Lord, have compassion on those who have fallen, and be moved with a zeal to make a difference in the lives of those who have spotted their garments.

Let's look at the ability to "build up." The word *build* is an architectural word that means "to cause a building to stand." It means "to lay a good foundation." In the natural realm, it is always important to leave yourself the ability to add on to your building in case you need to expand in the future. If you have outgrown your spiritual house, the Holy Ghost gives you the resources to add on to meet your demands.

If you have more ministry, then you have a place to house it, to build on. Are there weak areas in the structure? Build them up. You do this by praying in the Holy Spirit. This will build up your faith so that you can stand against Goliath and know that your God is bigger than the giant who defies you.

When God got ready to bless Elijah, His ultimate will was for the prophet to stand on Mt. Carmel, which means fruitful ground. But the blessing came progressively as he went to the brook Cherith where he drank from its waters and was fed by ravens. One day, however, the brook dried up and no longer met his needs. The word *Cherith* means to make covenant with. God made a covenant, proving not only Himself to Elijah, but Elijah to Himself.

Next, God sent Elijah to a widow in Zarephath, which means to refine as in a melting pot. Gold is not pure in its original form and must be refined, which is done by heating it to melting. The heat separates the raw substance from its impurities, which float to the surface and are skimmed off. God does the same for us, using the heat of trials to separate the gold from the dross in our lives.

God leads you through a progressive path, but the ultimate goal is to be on Mt. Carmel and be fruitful. He wants you to be able to call fire down from Heaven, to see into the Spirit as Elijah saw, and to persevere in prayer until God intervenes in your situation. The answer to your drought may appear to be a cloud the size of a man's hand, but you know a refreshing rain is about to fall.

Call down fire from Heaven!

This is why Christians from all denominations are being filled with the Holy Ghost. Having outgrown the tradition of their past experiences, they have passed the tests at Cherith and Zarephath and are ready to go to Mt. Carmel.

If you feel a hunger to go on with God, the Holy Ghost is telling you that your present spiritual house is too small. He is urging you to build upon your present foundation. In order to do this, however, we must pray in the Holy Ghost.

More Benefits

Unlike giving a message in tongues in a public meeting, which edifies other people, praying in tongues edifies you. We often walk into a nice church building, recognizing it as being a tremendous edifice. It simply means a great place for dwelling, meeting, communing, and fellowship.

Praying in tongues does at least five things for you individually:

1. It gives you the ability to talk to God alone, frustrating the devil.

"He that speaketh in an unknown tongue speaketh not unto men, but unto God" (1 Cor. 14:2). This gives you the ability to bypass all others and go into the presence of God. The Old Testament equivalent would be to go into the holy of holies and commune directly with God.

Your adversary brings certain things against you to discourage and cause you to lose focus. Praying in tongues enables us to bypass his radar system.

There are two great weapons in modern day warfare. One is the ability to fly fighter jets and bombers without being detected by radar. This is done by stealth bombers. Stealth means to have the ability to go unde-tected by enemy radar.

The second is the ability to jam the radar by sending a false signal. As you pray in the Spirit and shout your way through your storm, this sends a signal to the devil that totally jams his radar system.

2. It edifies the person praying (1 Cor. 14:4).

The word *edify* means "to build up, to build on, to establish a structure." As you pray in tongues, you enlarge your borders. If you have more ministry than prayer life, then add on. If you have outgrown where you are, then add on.

Add on!

Your complexes will vanish as the Holy Ghost imparts confidence. Your fears will vanish as the Holy Ghost builds you up. Your past failures and sins will be dealt a decisive blow by the Holy Ghost. This change will take every weak area in your structure and begin to brace and strengthen it, giving you glorious victory.

You may not even notice the change taking place, and you might not even realize it's the Holy Ghost doing the work quietly and internally. But it won't be long before what is happening on the inside begins to manifest itself on the outside. As you learn to pray in the Holy Ghost, it will just happen automatically.

As you come into a deeper relationship with God, you will find that you cannot survive on a "now I lay me down to sleep" prayer. Your prayer life will have to match your ministry and commitment to Spirit-filled living.

> *But ye, beloved, building up yourselves on your most holy faith, praying in the Holy Ghost* (Jude 20).

Praying in the Holy Ghost shores up the foundation of our faith.

The best defense against disease is our natural immune system, which has been designed by God to help us ward off the enemies of our body and diseases that come against us. But the immune system must be kept strong and vibrant by eating right, getting plenty of rest, and exercising.

Many of us are at our own lowest ebb spiritually and have become susceptible to anything that comes our way. But if we pray in the Holy Ghost, we will be built up, enabling us to fight off sin and discouragement.

> *And take the helmet of salvation, and the sword of the Spirit, which is the word of God: praying always with all prayer and supplication in the Spirit, and watching thereunto*

*with all perseverance and supplication for all
saints* (Ephesians 6:17-18).

Many Christians feel this spiritual preparation is like
choosing their clothes for the day from their closet. The
apostle Paul mentioned our warfare, our enemies, and our
armor, which covers every vital part of a soldier: the helmet
(our mind); the breastplate (our heart); the girdle of truth
(the truth of God's Word upon which the hole armor rests);
the shield of faith, which kept the soldier walking forward
and never turning his back, which was exposed; the preparation of the gospel on our feet (our walk).

This armor dresses us for any occasion. But the key
is in verses 17 and 18. After describing the armor piece
by piece, Paul goes right from verse 17 to verse 18 without stopping. It's as if he's saying, "This is how you get
the armor: praying always in the Spirit." Praying in the
Holy Ghost clothes us from head to foot with the armor
of God. Yes, praying in the Spirit arms you with an arsenal that will cause you to stand. Hallelujah for the ability
to pray in the Holy Ghost!

4. *It builds up a wall of defense.*

> *When the enemy shall come in like a flood,
> the Spirit of the Lord shall lift up a standard
> against him* (Isaiah 59:19).

Yes, there are times when the enemy invades our
lives. He will come into your mind; he will come into

your marriage; he will come into your ministry. He comes in like a flood and desires to devour you and anything that has been born of God in your life.

The Holy Spirit stands by as your ally. When the enemy comes in like a flood, the Spirit shall lift up a standard against him. He provides you with a place of defense, a place of shelter, a place of refuge, a place to hide.

Job's life is a good example of this. When God praised Job's integrity, satan pointed out:

> *Hast not thou made an hedge about him,*
> *and about his house, and about all that he*
> *hath on every side?* (Job 1:10) *The adversary*
> *asked permission to touch all that Job had.*
> *Satan came in like a flood, destroying his*
> *sons, daughters, servants, and livestock. Not*
> *satisfied with this, satan asked permission*
> *to afflict Job's body. God set a limit, however,*
> *and said, "Save his life"* (Job 2:6).

Praying in the Spirit sets up a wall of defense that satan cannot penetrate. The Spirit will lift up the wall of the blood of Jesus and say, "satan, you can't touch this!"

5. It helps you relieve anxiety.

> *Come ye yourselves apart into a desert*
> *place, and rest a while* (Mark 6:31).

Praying in the Spirit allows you to come apart before you fall apart. Many of you are under severe pressure. You are tense, battle weary. Like the disciples, you need a solitary place to rest awhile.

Praying in the Spirit pulls us into an experience with God. It's not surprising that Paul wondered whether he was in the body or out of the body. The apostle saw and heard things unlawful for a man to speak. God in the Spirit takes us to paradise, pulling us apart from the pressures of the world before we come apart.

A piece of material does not come apart suddenly. It unravels bit by bit. If you don't repair it, a small tear can cause the whole garment to come apart.

Praying in the Spirit brings us to that solitary place with God to help cope with stress, pressure, and anxiety. If your life is falling apart, your need is similar to the woman with the issue of blood. She wanted to touch the hem of Christ's garment. She realized the hem was where all loose ends were put back together. This is what praying in the Spirit will do.

Praying in the Spirit brings peace.

What is it then? I will pray with the spirit,
and I will pray with the understanding also:
I will sing with the spirit, and I will sing

ANOINTING FALL ON ME

with the understanding also (1 Corinthians
14:15).

"I will pray with the spirit" means that you rely on
the Holy Ghost to guide you as you pray. He will speak,
but we must listen. When we pray with the Spirit, we are
praying with the knowledge of God's will:

> *Likewise the Spirit also helpeth our infirmi-*
> *ties: for we know not what we should pray for*
> *as we ought: but the Spirit itself maketh inter-*
> *cession for us with groanings which cannot be*
> *uttered* (Romans 8:26).

We also pray with the insight of the Spirit:

> *And he that searcheth the hearts knoweth*
> *what is the mind of the Spirit, because he*
> *maketh intercession for the saints according*
> *to the will of God* (Romans 8:27).

When we pray in the Spirit, we pray with fervency
and intensity as the Spirit gives us the unction to focus
on what we are praying for and diligently seek God.

> *But without faith it is impossible to please*
> *him: for he that cometh to God must believe*
> *that he is, and that he is a rewarder of them*
> *that diligently seek him* (Hebrews 11:6).

"I will pray with the understanding" means that as we pray by the unction and leadership of the Holy Ghost, we pray a prayer that will have meaning as the same Holy Ghost interprets to us the things that we have spoken.

Sometimes we have no knowledge of how to pray because the things that we confront are bigger than we are.

They are deeper than our human logic can comprehend.

That's why we need to pray within the spirit realm, which is bigger than any problem, weakness, or dilemma we face. We also need to ask God to interpret to us the things that we have spoken through the auspice of the Holy Ghost. As He reveals them to us, we will gain an understanding.

We Need the Anointing

Sometimes we don't know what to say. Our heart is crushed; our spirit is overwhelmed. We know that we need a touch; we know the area that needs to be touched, but we don't always know what to say.

Have you ever been so overwhelmed, so overcome that all you can do is groan? Maybe you can only say, "Jesus, help me," or "I need You, Lord." That's when we need to change our language. We need to wait on the Holy Ghost because He knows how to pray—and what to pray. The Holy Ghost will always pray in alignment with the will of God (Rom. 8:27).

Help me, Jesus!

The anointing of the Holy Ghost doesn't always bring chills or goose bumps. It isn't always charged with emotion. The anointing, however, brings power.

The Old Testament high priest knew there was only one place where he could see and experience a manifestation of God's glory and that was in the holy of holies. That's where God promised to show Himself and commune with His people (Exod. 25:17-22).

In these last days, satan and all his cohorts are waging a final onslaught against the Church. We must know God in a way in which we have never known Him before. Within some of you are miracles, unborn babies, ministries, and gifts. Many of you have callings on your life.

Because of circumstances—perhaps something beyond your control; perhaps because of your faults, failures, or your past life—satan has told you that your baby, your gift, your ministry must be aborted. But satan is a liar. Scripture tells us *the gifts and calling of God are without repentance* (Rom. 11:29). You need to get to where you can see the raw, undiluted presence of God and His anointing.

You Can Make It!

What encourages me when I go through the storms of life? I look in the Word of God and find that someone else has already been there and made it through. We are surrounded by witnesses:

> *Wherefore seeing we also are compassed about with so great a cloud of witnesses, let us lay aside every weight, and the sin which doth so easily beset us, and let us run with patience the race that is set before us* (Hebrews 12:1).

In each instance, however, these saints had to get to a certain place before they saw the manifestation of God.

Noah endured a torrential downpour that flooded the earth for months, but he had a place that gave him access to God. On the third level of the ark a window gave him access to the heavenlies.

> *A window shalt thou make to the ark, and in a cubit shalt thou finish it above; and the door of the ark shalt thou set in the side thereof; with lower, second, and third stories shalt thou make it* (Genesis 6:16).

In the midst of his storm he found solace and peace.

Jacob struggled for years with who he was compared to who he wanted to be. His wrestling climaxed when he got to Jabbok, which means to pour out, to empty.

Jacob went alone to Jabbok, the place of struggle where he wrestled with an angel. Divinity met with humanity, and Jacob's thigh was put out of joint. Upon arriving at the place, the patriarch was Jacob (swindler, supplanter, cheater), but after the struggle, his name was Israel (prince of God). It was a place of power, as God gave him power with Himself and man (Gen. 32:21-29).

Moses struggled with his leadership responsibilities over the nation of Israel. The demands of the multitude taxed Moses to the point of exhaustion. Moses asked God for a manifestation of His glory. But before Moses could see this manifestation, he had to get to a certain place. Hidden in the cleft of a rock, Moses saw the afterglow of God's glory, but only after he got to that place.

How the Anointing Works

If you're a believer in Christ, you have some type of calling on your life. You may be a pastor or a leader in the church. You may have a specific gift that needs to be stirred up.

You have a calling.

Like Jacob, you may be struggling with who you are. Some of you may be wrestling with your past. You need to know that there is a place with God of yoke-breaking anointing. Let's look at two passages of Scripture for some timely truths:

> *Behold, how good and how pleasant it is for brethren to dwell together in unity! It is like the precious ointment upon the head, that ran down upon the beard, even Aaron's beard: that went down to the skirts of his garments; as the dew of Hermon, and as the dew that descended upon the mountains of Zion: for there the Lord commanded the blessing, even life for evermore* (Psalm 133:1-3).

> *And it shall come to pass in that day, that his burden shall be taken away from off thy shoulder, and his yoke from off thy neck, and the yoke shall be destroyed because of the anointing* (Isaiah 10:27).

1. The anointing flows from the head down (Ps. 133:2). Jesus is the head. His anointing is flowing, but we must be in alignment (in fellowship) with Him.

2. The anointing will be *"as the dew of Hermon"* (Ps. 133:3a). The Israelites knew the dew of Mt. Hermon and Mt. Zion was heavy even in dry weather.

3. The anointing will take authority over your situations. *"For there the Lord commanded the blessing"* (Ps. 133:3b).

4. The anointing will lift burdens from your shoulder (Isa. 10:27a).

5. The anointing will take away yokes that have caused you to say and do things and go places you really didn't desire (Isa. 10:27).

6. The anointing will destroy the yoke. It isn't enough to just lift the yoke from your neck. If you leave a yoke enabled, it can resume its previous position at any time. The anointing dismantles everything that satan had planned for your life.

In the days of the judges, the Philistines stole the ark of the covenant. They placed the ark beside their god Dagon. The presence of God in the ark caused Dagon to fall on his face. After the Philistines sat him up again, the presence of God caused Dagon to fall a second time. Upon his second fall his head was cut off and also both palms (1 Sam. 5:1-4).

Everything satan planned to do (his head) and all the things he wanted to do (his hands) has been destroyed by the anointing. He has been cut off and rendered helpless.

No weapon that is formed against thee shall prosper; and every tongue that shall rise against thee in judgment thou shalt condemn. This is the heritage of the servants of the Lord, and their righteousness is of me, saith the Lord (Isaiah 54:17).

This level of anointing is vital because we will need to have high-level talks with God that we do not want satan to hear or to understand. We need the ability to change languages. Tongues are available, and they are for you. You can speak the language as the Spirit of God gives the utterance.

The Master Key

As long as we operate according to human logic and our carnal perceptions of things, we will find ourselves up and down with our circumstances. But when we tap into the Holy Ghost, our knowledge takes on a whole new perspective and we begin to operate in Kingdom authority.

Tap into the Holy Ghost for wisdom.

We no longer fret when the gates of hell rise up against us because we know that Jesus has given us the master key, which is the anointing of the Holy Ghost. You don't have to worry about being locked in or locked out if you have the master key. The master key can open any lock.

Jesus told Peter not to worry about the gates of hell because He would give him the keys to the Kingdom (Matt. 16:17-19). These keys were a mystery to others, but to Peter the keys solved any dilemma because they were Kingdom keys. They were a mystery to some, but a message of prevailing authority to those who understand the code.

Jesus faced these four dilemmas:

1. Traditions of men (Matt. 15:1-3).

2. Outward religion that left the heart desperately wicked (Matt. 15:10-20).

3. Physical infirmities, a type of spiritual handicaps (Matt. 15:29-31).

4. Physical hunger, a type of spiritual starvation and famine (Matt. 15:32-39).

Jesus asked His disciples, *"Whom do men say that I the Son of man am?"* (Matt. 16:13). Understanding the answer to this question opened the way to an anointing that left the gates of hell powerless.

They answered:

> *Some say that thou art John the Baptist:*
> *some, Elias; and others, Jeremias, or one of*
> *the prophets* (Matthew 16:14).

These were merely fleshly men with limitations.

Then Jesus asked, *"But whom say ye that I am?"* (Matt. 16:15). Peter confessed, *"Thou art the Christ, the Son of the living God"* (Matt. 16:16). The Greek word is *Christos*, the anointed one from God.

Jesus knew these four types of crises had left the people in hopeless situations. They were trying to handle these four areas by seeing Jesus as just an earthly man, a teacher, or a prophet. These four dilemmas had left them victims locked in a prison without a key.

When we recognize Jesus as the Christ, however, He gives us a master key (the anointing) to unlock any crisis in our life. The anointing does not promise to keep the gates of hell from coming against you, but it prevents the gates of hell from prevailing against you.

Everything Has a Price

When you shop, you know that everything has a price tag. As you peruse the merchandise in stores, you probably ask yourself some very basic questions:

1. Do I need this particular item?

2. Can I afford the price?

3. Does it have a warranty with it?

4. Would I use it if I bought it?

The anointing falls under these same four guidelines.

1. You desperately need the anointing of the Holy Ghost.

2. The Holy Ghost is well worth the price.

3. The Holy Ghost has a warranty sealed unto the day of redemption.

4. In order to fulfill everything that a sovereign God has ordained for your life, you must use the power of the Holy Ghost to reach your potential and destiny.

Jesus Christ knew the importance of being anointed for works of service. He quoted the prophet Isaiah at the outset of His ministry:

The Spirit of the Lord God is upon me; because the Lord hath anointed me to preach good tidings unto the meek; he hath sent me to bind up the brokenhearted, to proclaim liberty to the captives, and the opening of the prison to them that are bound; to proclaim the acceptable year of the Lord, and the day of vengeance of our God; to comfort all that mourn; to appoint unto them that mourn in Zion, to give unto them beauty for ashes, the oil of joy for mourning, the garment of praise for the spirit of heaviness; that they might be called trees of righteousness, the planting of the Lord, that he might be glorified (Isaiah 61:1-3).

May we cry out for an infilling of the Holy Ghost that we might be enabled to pray in the Spirit and walk in a greater anointing. Like our Master, may we be anointed *"with the Holy Ghost and with power"* (Acts 10:38).

Cry out for a Holy Ghost infilling.

Thoughts and Reflections

_____

_____

_____

_____

_____

_____

ANOINTING FALL ON ME

CHAPTER 4

SECRET CODE

God has spoken to His people from the very beginning:

> *And they heard the voice of the Lord God*
> *walking in the garden in the cool of the day:*
> *and Adam and his wife hid themselves from*
> *the presence of the Lord God amongst the*
> *trees of the garden* (Genesis 3:8).

He communicated His desire for them to keep the garden, to be fruitful and multiply, and not to eat of the tree of the knowledge of good and evil.

God spoke to His people through the prophets:

God, who at sundry times and in divers manners spake in time past unto the fathers by the prophets (Hebrews 1:1).

He also spoke to us by His Son:

Hath in these last days spoken unto us by his Son, whom he hath appointed heir of all things, by whom also he made the worlds (Hebrews 1:2).

He spoke to us by miracles:

God also bearing them witness, both with signs and wonders, and with divers miracles, and gifts of the Holy Ghost, according to his own will? (Hebrews 2:4)

He then spoke by His apostles. As a result of the mighty outpouring at Pentecost, God said He would speak through His Spirit:

And it shall come to pass afterward, that I will pour out my spirit upon all flesh; and your sons and your daughters shall prophesy, your old men shall dream dreams, your young men shall see visions (Joel 2:28).

Many try to limit God, saying He has spoken in the past but has ceased to speak today. This, however, is not true. God continues to speak to us through His written Word.

The Holy Ghost also speaks to us today. Tongues are God's message for the last days. It isn't the only way that He can speak, but it is one avenue of speech. We need faith to allow Him to speak and interpret the message through a willing vessel.

The issue in biblical times and today is this: Can you hear what God is saying? God is certainly speaking:

> *He that hath an ear, let him hear what the Spirit saith unto the churches; He that overcometh shall not be hurt of the second death* (Revelation 2:11).

> *Howbeit when he, the Spirit of truth, is come, he will guide you into all truth: for he shall not speak of himself; but whatsoever he shall hear, that shall he speak: and he will shew you things to come* (John 16:13).

We need to get hold of God like never before because He is speaking a vital message in these last days. He is looking for someone to deliver a timely, life-changing word. Many times, however, it is in secret code and can only be understood by those who have the Holy Ghost.

> *Surely the Lord God will do nothing, but he revealeth his secret unto his servants the prophets* (Amos 3:7).

> *The secret things belong unto the Lord our God: but those things which are revealed*

belong unto us and to our children for ever,
that we may do all the words of this law
(Deuteronomy 29:29).

A judge named Ehud had a message, which he called "a secret errand," to deliver to the king (Judg. 3:19).

These three verses show us some interesting things:

1. God has some secrets (Deut. 29:29).

2. He reveals these secrets to His servants (Amos 3:7).

3. God looks for willing servants to deliver these secret messages.

Every message has certain components:

1. A person who sends the message.

2. A person who receives the message.

3. A third party who may be involved because the person sending the message cannot always contact the primary party directly. In this case, he or she contacts someone who will deliver the message.

4. The interpretation of the message conveys what is meant by the person sending it. The message must be made plain and spoken in a way that can be understood.

Why Secret Code?

Why should God speak in secret code, and to whom is He speaking? When God speaks in secret, He does so for at least two reasons:

1. God wants to have an intimate relationship with you. You tell your secrets and innermost thoughts only to your closest, most trusted friends.

2. By speaking in secret code, God insures that the devil does not understand the strategy of the church. This enables us to make an unannounced surprise attack because the secret code bypasses the radar and defense system of the satanic forces in opposition to us (Eph. 6:12).

Mysteries of the Kingdom

If ye love me, keep my commandments. And I will pray the Father, and he shall give you another Comforter, that he may abide with you for ever; even the Spirit of truth; whom the world cannot receive, because it seeth him not, neither knoweth him: but ye know him; for he dwelleth with you, and shall be in you. I will not leave you comfortless: I will come to you. Yet a little while, and the world

*seeth me no more; but ye see me: because I
live, ye shall live also. At that day ye shall
know that I am in my Father, and ye in me,
and I in you* (John 14:15-20).

This Scripture indicates the Kingdom of God was
going through some drastic changes.

1. We find the changing of the guard.

*"I will pray the Father, and he shall give you another
Comforter"* (vs. 16). *Another* in this passage means
"another one just like me." Jesus confirmed this in the
very next verse: *"Ye know him* [the Spirit of truth]; *for he
dwelleth with you, and shall be in you"* (vs. 17).

2. We find an obligation on our part to receive the Holy Ghost.

Jesus said, *"If ye love me, keep my commandments"*
(vs. 15). As a result of our walking in obedience, Jesus
said that He would pray to the Father. He in turn would
send another Comforter to us.

3. Jesus said three things about the Holy Ghost in John 14:17.

- The world cannot receive Him.
- The world cannot see Him, because His ways are not their ways; He is a mystery to them.
- The world doesn't know Him.

All the miracles of Christ declared what His followers would do in that day. Because the world did not receive Him, did not see Him, and did not know Him, they crucified the Lord of glory. Only Christ's inner circle of Peter, James, and John witnessed His transfiguration (Matt. 17:1-9). Only these three saw the inner turmoil of Jesus as He poured out His soul in prayer and conformed to the Father's will in the Garden of Gethsemane (Matt. 26:37-44). Only John went to the cross. Is it any wonder that he received an amazing vision known as "The Revelation of Jesus Christ"? Before receiving this vision, he was exiled to the isle of Patmos. Jesus spoke mysteries to His beloved friend John that still perplex the world—and even the Church. In order to receive this surpassing revelation, John had to detach himself from earthly things. He heard a voice say, *"Come up hither, and I will shew thee things which must be hereafter"* (Rev. 4:1).

God calls those who are committed to excellence to a place of seclusion and aloneness. The Holy Ghost is saying, "Detach yourself from things that blind you from seeing My mysteries and deafen you from hearing My language."

Jesus is speaking, but even those in the Church are missing Him because they do not hear His language. Many are not hearing His voice because tradition has left them content with only the first glimpse of His glory. The glory of Christ far exceeds any glory ever known by man. In those three short years Jesus began to reveal the mysteries of a powerful Kingdom that was greater than any problem, sickness, or dilemma.

Jesus is speaking—listen.

They Didn't Understand Him

Why did the people crucify the Prince of Glory? Jesus Christ had a message, power, and authority that frightened the religious hierarchy of His day. Yes, He was a Jew who spoke the regional dialect. But sometimes He also spoke mysteries to His disciples. Thousands followed Christ, but He handpicked twelve to be with Him.

Why aren't more believers hearing from God? Many are not walking in obedience and do not have the fullness of the Holy Ghost. Jesus only reveals His secrets to those who are trustworthy and have intimate fellowship with Him.

Jesus told His disciples that the world would not understand, see, or know, but those who had the Holy Ghost would.

> *Yet a little while, and the world seeth me no more; but ye see me: because I live, ye shall live also. At that day ye shall know that I am in my Father, and ye in me, and I in you* (John 14:19-20).

He was saying, "In that day they will see me as dead, but you will know that I am still in control. When they bury Me in a tomb, some will say it's over. But you will know I spoke mysteries the world could not understand. 'Destroy this temple and in three days I will raise it up.' When they come on that first Easter morning and find My body gone, they will say it was stolen. You will know that I have risen from the dead. My ministry will continue through the Holy Ghost."

"*At that day ye shall know*" (John 14:20) denotes something progressive. "*Then shall we know, if we follow on to know the Lord*" (Hos. 6:3). "*Ye shall know the truth*" (John 8:32). "*When I became a man*" (1 Cor. 13:11) denotes something that isn't complete but is in the making.

Surpassing Our Intellect

The apostle Paul wrote about Kingdom revelation that staggers the mind. The truth is spoken and revealed in secret code. We must understand the code.

> *But as it is written, Eye hath not seen, nor ear heard, neither have entered into the heart of man, the things which God hath prepared for them that love him. But God hath revealed them unto us by his Spirit: for the Spirit searcheth all things, yea, the deep things of God* (1 Corinthians 2:9-10).

1. The code is being spoken. "*But God hath revealed*" (vs.10a).

2. The code speaks *"the deep things of God"*—the mysteries of the Kingdom (vs. 10b).

3. The code speaks only to those who have an intimate relationship with God. *"The things which God hath prepared for them that love him"* (vs. 9b).

4. The code speaks things that our carnal nature can neither attain nor perceive. Carnality cannot see. *"Eye hath not seen."* Carnality cannot hear. *"Ear hath not heard."* Carnality cannot feel. *"Neither have entered into the heart of man"* (vs. 9a).

A Product of Our Environment

Wherefore, my beloved, as ye have always obeyed, not as in my presence only, but now much more in my absence, work out your own salvation with fear and trembling. For it is God which worketh in you both to will and to do of his good pleasure (Philippians 2:12-13).

This passage of Scripture shows us two things:

1. Things will begin to work their way out. *"Work out your own salvation"* (vs. 12).

2. The things which work out do so as a result of things working in. *"For it is God which worketh in"* (vs. 13). If you stay around something—be it good or bad—eventually you will begin to resemble it.

Noah's ark looked the same on the outside as on the inside. God told Noah, *"pitch it within* [inside] *and without* [outside] *with pitch"* (Gen. 6:14). Pitch is a sealant. God wants to do a work beginning inside you until it also manifests outwardly in the form of signs.

> *Open yourself to God's word in you.*

> *And these signs shall follow them that believe;*
> *In my name shall they cast out devils; they*
> *shall speak with new tongues* (Mark 16:17).

Jesus wants the church to become so attached to His anointing and so detached from the world that we begin to resemble the Kingdom.

> *For the kingdom of God is not meat and*
> *drink; but righteousness, and peace, and*
> *joy in the Holy Ghost* (Romans 14:17).

As the Kingdom of God functions in the mystery of the Holy Ghost, it will become something that far exceeds a group of rituals, traditions, ceremonies, rules, and guidelines.

As we get in tune with the voice of the Spirit, we begin to produce the fruit of the Spirit. The fruit of the Spirit is nothing more than the Church falling in love with Jesus and becoming impregnated with His seed (the Word). This will produce the fruit of the Spirit. First, however, we must have an intimate relationship with God.

Do You Know Jesus?

First, do you know Him in the pardon and forgiveness of your sins? Second, do you know Him intimately? Has your relationship with Jesus grown to the point at which you both recognize Him and produce His offspring (the fruit of the Spirit)?

We find this truth throughout Scripture. After creating the first couple, God said, *"Therefore shall a man... cleave unto his wife: and they shall be one flesh"* (Gen. 2:24). Adam and Eve were together and knew each other. *"And Adam knew Eve his wife; and she conceived"* (Gen. 4:1). *"And Cain knew his wife; and she conceived"* (Gen. 4:17). *"And Adam knew his wife again; and she bare a son"* (Gen. 4:25).

After the angel announced to Mary that she had been favored to conceive and bear God's Son, a startled young virgin asked, *"How shall this be, seeing I know not a man?"* (Luke 1:34).

These Scriptures bring out one point: you cannot produce offspring without intimacy. Many Christians have had spiritual orgasms but have never conceived the seed of God's Word. In order for us to bring forth Kingdom offspring, we must know the King of the Kingdom.

Jesus said:

> *At that day ye shall know that I am in my Father, and ye in me, and I in you* (John 14:20).

We need to know the Lord Jesus in a spiritually intimate way. The only way to know Him is to be filled with the Holy Ghost. As we walk in what we know, our outward person begins to resemble our inward being.

Salt and Light

As the Church allows the Holy Ghost to work in and through us, the world will begin to see Jesus and the Kingdom of God in action. It will be a mystery to the world but a powerful reality to the Church. But it won't happen overnight. It's progressive, day by day, trial by trial, storm by storm, valley by valley, and temptation by temptation.

When Jesus was on earth, He said:

> *Then spake Jesus again unto them, saying, I am the light of the world: he that followeth*

me shall not walk in darkness, but shall have the light of life (John 8:12).

But when He died, darkness covered the earth. Except for the Holy Ghost, darkness would prevail. But as the Body of Christ allows the Holy Ghost to fill every fiber of their being, we become the light of the world.

We are a beacon, a lighthouse to a world of storm-tossed, beaten, battered individuals. We are to be a city set on a hill and illuminated by the Holy Ghost. Our joy, our peace, our righteousness should shine brightly, encouraging others to find a refuge in our God. The fruit of the Spirit in our lives will act as a magnet and draw them to Jesus.

Be a beacon for the dark world.

When Jesus walked the earth, He was a preservative for this world. A thief could not die without first being preserved by His forgiveness; a widow's only son, the apple of her eye, could not reach the gates of death without Jesus stopping the funeral procession. Lazarus could not lie decomposing in a tomb without hearing a voice, "Lazarus, come forth" (John 11:43)!

As the Church comes into a Kingdom relationship with Jesus, we then become preservatives:

Ye are the salt of the earth: but if the salt have lost his savour, wherewith shall it be salted? it is thenceforth good for nothing, but to be cast out, and to be trodden under foot of men (Matthew 5:13).

Salt does several things:

1. It creates thirst.
2. It preserves.
3. If poured into wounds, it will burn.
4. If spread by shaking, it will season.

We need to allow the Holy Ghost to saturate our very being so we become sons of God who carry on the Kingdom work.

God Has Your Number

The gift of tongues can be understood by using the telephone as an analogy. One party calls in; the other party receives. This gives you a twofold ability to call sometimes and to hear sometimes.

God is ringing your telephone today. He may have to call you to give you a message for someone else who, for one reason or another, cannot hear. The only way the message can get through is for you to speak out what God has spoken into your spirit. Be sure to pray for an interpreter.

God does the calling and you do the receiving. Remember, sometimes certain parties cannot be reached so the caller will contact you to pass on the message. God may call other parties, but for one reason or another they do not hear.

Sometimes they are out of the calling area (too far from God). Sometimes they give God a busy signal (too occupied for God). Sometimes they simply won't answer (too disrespectful toward God). When this happens, God dials your number and gives you a message in a heavenly language that can be interpreted.

Many anointed people wrongly believe that their anointing gives them the right to get out of order. They may exercise their gift, but the message of God is misrepresented, wrong, or even damaging. This confuses and wounds people.

Your anointing does not give you the right to come in and wreck a service:

And the spirits of the prophets are subject to the prophets (1 Corinthians 14:32).

When a true manifestation of God comes with a message in tongues, we need to pray for the interpretation, which is just as important as the message; otherwise, how will the people understand? If this does not come, then someone is out of order:

For God is not the author of confusion, but of peace, as in all churches of the saints (1 Corinthians 14:33).

Timeliness is another important issue with the gift of tongues. Your anointing may not always be in dispute as much as your timing. If your message is not given in its proper timing, it can hurt, confuse, and mislead.

The Holy Spirit is not unseemly. He does not cause disorder.

Timeliness is key.

The Corinthian church didn't have a problem with spirituality, but with order. There must be a balance. We need Spirit-filled churches, but we also need Word-filled churches that have the wisdom to know how to function.

Is it any wonder that satan battles the gifts and manifestations of the Holy Ghost? He knows the gifts of the Spirit are going to cause the Church to perform signs, bringing the gospel to our troubled, chaotic society.

God said:

The people that do know their God shall be strong, and do exploits (Daniel 11:32).

God is looking for a Church that believes He can confirm them and their ministry with gifts, signs, and wonders in the Holy Ghost. (See Hebrews 2:3-4 and Mark 16:17-18.)

Don't be dismayed if those who see you say, "These people are fanatics!" The Holy Ghost will cause a division between truth and falsehood.

When you begin to function in the gift of God for your life and the devil sees a true manifestation of the Holy Ghost, expect to be put on the devil's hit list. This is nothing more than a trick of the enemy to get you to stop.

The God Who Shows Up

In the Old Testament, God would just show up with a message and say, "Let it be," and it was so. God will step in just when you think He won't, just when you need Him, just in time. What was the difference between the God of Elijah and the god of the prophets of Baal? The God of Elijah showed up.

> *And call ye on the name of your gods, and I will call on the name of the Lord: and the God that answereth by fire, let him be God. And all the people answered and said, It is well spoken* (1 Kings 18:24).

Now if God appeared on the scene for a prophet who had only the blood of an animal sacrifice, how much more will He appear for those who have the blood of Jesus and the baptism of the Holy Ghost?

> *Then the king sent unto him a captain of fifty with his fifty. And he went up to him: and, behold, he sat on the top of an hill. And he spake unto him, Thou man of God, the king hath said, Come down* (2 Kings 1:9).

When the king sent a captain of fifty to Elijah, he confronted the prophet. Elijah refused to come down and replied:

> *And Elijah answered and said to the captain of fifty, If I be a man of God, then let fire come down from heaven, and consume thee and thy fifty. And there came down fire from heaven, and consumed him and his fifty* (2 Kings 1:10).

The fire of God consumed this messenger and his fifty, then another captain with his fifty.

We need to have the same spirit as Elijah. When tempted to align ourselves with the world, we must tell the devil, "I cannot and will not come down!" All too often people are so close to the devil that they are not intimidating his kingdom at all. But when the Kingdom of light stands in unity, the kingdom of darkness comes down.

> ## *Kingdom light destroys kingdom darkness.*

> *And Jesus knew their thoughts, and said unto them, Every kingdom divided against itself is brought to desolation; and every city or house divided against itself shall not stand* (Matthew 12:25).

Many church folks have followed the path of society. We live in a fast-food world where nobody wants to wait. Even church people want a quick fix. We want power without pursuing the power giver. But anyone who has ever been mightily anointed of God has had to pursue God.

> *As the hart panteth after the water brooks, so panteth my soul after thee, O God. My soul thirsteth for God, for the living God: when shall I come and appear before God?* (Psalm 42:1-2)

The Holy Ghost Doesn't Speak His Own Agenda

> *Howbeit when he, the Spirit of truth, is come, he will guide you into all truth: for he shall not speak of himself; but whatsoever he shall*

hear, that shall he speak: and he will shew
you things to come (John 16:13).

This verse gives us some insight regarding the ministry of the Holy Spirit.

1. One day the Holy Spirit would reign in authority. *"When he, the Spirit of truth, is come"* signified a day when He would arrive to minister and reign in authority.

2. *"He will guide you into all truth."* The ministry of the Holy Spirit involves guidance, but the guidance is the truth of God's Word. Jesus said, *"And ye shall know the truth, and the truth shall make you free"* (John 8:32).

3. The Holy Spirit does not come to fulfill His own agenda. *"For he shall not speak of himself."*

4. The Holy Spirit listens before He speaks. *"But whatsoever he shall hear, that shall he speak."* The Holy Ghost listens from the portals of glory to hear the will of God. This is why we must listen before we speak as the Holy Spirit gives utterance. The Holy Spirit pleads, with groanings, the will of God for our life.

Sometimes He dials our number to give someone else a message. Have you ever answered the phone and learned the caller wanted to speak to someone else? We usually ask, "Who is this?" and "May I take a message?"

The Holy Spirit may be calling that person, but He isn't getting through. In this case, He may give us a message to relay to the other party. The Holy Ghost hears from Heaven and relays the message to someone who has the gift of tongues. Then we need to pray for someone to take the heavenly language and interpret it to the congregation.

Can You Hear the Holy Ghost?

God is definitely speaking to His people. The question is: Can we hear Him? The Holy Ghost is speaking right now. He is speaking words of truth and guidance. He speaks what He hears in Heaven.

Whenever the Holy Ghost speaks, He testifies that He has been in the boardroom of Heaven. Hearing from Him causes us to lift our head. Just when satan thought he had you, to his amazement you begin to shout. He doesn't know it, but you heard a word.

You may be going through a valley, but the Holy Ghost told you that Jesus is the Lily of the Valley. You may be going down a perplexing path, but you heard that Jesus is a Wonderful Counselor. You may be going through a famine in your life and ministry, but you heard a word that said, "Trust Me when you can't trace Me." You may be facing an insurmountable trial, but you heard a word that said, "Stand still and see the salvation of the Lord."

I heard a word, and you can too. Sometimes the word is for you, and sometimes it is for someone else. Sometimes God merely wants to use you as a spokesman.

Jonah's name means carrier pigeon. God had a message for him to deliver to a third party, the people of Nineveh.

Allow God to use you in the same way.

Seven Areas

Has someone ever tried to relay a message to you over the phone? The words they spoke weren't their own, but belonged to someone else. Someone gave them a message, and they in turn repeated what they heard.

In the same way the Holy Ghost has you on the line and speaks a word to you. It may not be a word directly from the Bible, but it is a *rhema* word designed to fit your crisis.

Remember that the Holy Ghost doesn't speak on His own initiative. He doesn't convey His own ideas or plans. He speaks only what He hears from Heaven.

> *Howbeit when he, the Spirit of truth, is come,*
> *he will guide you into all truth: for he shall*
> *not speak of himself; but whatsoever he shall*
> *hear, that shall he speak: and he will shew*
> *you things to come* (John 16:13).

Let's look at seven areas of your life in which the Holy Ghost wants to speak.

1. The Holy Ghost wants to speak to you things that go beyond human logic, natural tendency, and physical comprehension.

But as it is written, Eye hath not seen, nor ear heard, neither have entered into the heart of man, the things which God hath prepared for them that love him. But God hath revealed them unto us by his Spirit: for the Spirit searcheth all things, yea, the deep things of God (1 Corinthians 2:9-10).

In order for us to speak out revelations, we must first allow revelations to be spoken into our spirits.

But the natural man receiveth not the things of the Spirit of God: for they are foolishness unto him: neither can he know them, because they are spiritually discerned (1 Corinthians 2:14).

What the Spirit wants to speak and reveal goes beyond three of our five senses.

- Spiritual revelation goes beyond our seeing. *"Eye hath not seen"* (1 Cor. 2:9).

- What God wants to show us cannot be seen through our fleshly eyes.

- Spiritual revelation goes beyond our ability to hear. *"Ear hath not heard"* (1 Cor. 2:9). We need a spiritual ear to hear what the Spirit is saying to the church in these last days. (See Revelation 2:17.)

- Spiritual revelation goes beyond anything we have ever felt before. *"Neither have entered into the heart of man"* (1 Cor. 2:9). No matter how good we have ever felt in the Spirit, we have never reached the heights that raw spiritual revelation will give. How will you ever persuade people to see, hear, and feel the things of the Spirit if you are not sold on them yourself?

2. The Holy Ghost will testify to you. *"The Spirit itself beareth witness with our spirit, that we are the children of God"* (Rom. 8:16). Notice three things:

    - There is a testimony. *"The Spirit... beareth witness."* This means He testifies as one who stands as an eyewitness to corroborate your statement.

- He testifies to our spirit. He beareth witness *"with our spirit."* Our innermost being needs a testimony, for it is through our testimony that we overcome the devil.

- God doesn't delegate this important task. *"The Spirit itself"* speaks regarding our sonship and becoming joint heirs with Christ. (See Romans 8:17.) We are His beneficiaries. *"He* [the Holy Ghost] *shall take of mine, and shall shew it unto you"* (John 16:15). He witnesses that we are sons of God. Then He shows us what is ours because we're heirs.

3. The Holy Ghost will give you direction. Notice what the Spirit said to Philip: *"Go near, and join thyself to this chariot"* (Acts 8:29). Sometimes the message for yourself or others gives direction.

4. The Holy Ghost speaks to lead us to obedience (Acts 10:1-23). As Peter pondered a heavenly vision and wondered what it meant, the Holy Spirit spoke to him.

While Peter thought on the vision, the Spirit said unto him, Behold, three men seek thee. Arise therefore, and get thee down, and go with them, doubting nothing: for I have sent them (Acts 10:19-20).

Despite the vision, Peter was walking in prejudicial disobedience until the Holy Ghost spoke. His words broke down the barriers of racism, religion, and prejudice.

5. The Holy Ghost shows you God's choice for companionship.

As they ministered to the Lord, and fasted, the Holy Ghost said, Separate me Barnabas and Saul for the work whereunto I have called them (Acts 13:2).

This verse focused on two partners in ministry, but the voice of the Holy Spirit can have an illuminating impact on selecting a partner for marriage or business.

6. The Holy Ghost will speak and close doors that were the right thing but the wrong time.

Now when they had gone throughout Phrygia and the region of Galatia, and were forbidden of the Holy Ghost to preach the word in Asia, after they were come to Mysia, they assayed to go into Bithynia: but the Spirit suffered them not (Acts 16:6-7).

Paul and Silas were doing the right thing, but it wasn't timely. Unknown to these apostles, a man was crying out desperately for help in Macedonia. The Holy Ghost prioritized Philippi over Galatia and Bithynia because of the need in one man's life.

7. The Holy Ghost sometimes warns us.

And finding disciples, we tarried there seven days: who said to Paul through the Spirit, that he should not go up to Jerusalem (Acts 21:4).

If we listen to the warnings of the Holy Ghost, we will avoid many difficulties and snares.

The Holy Ghost speaks for a variety of reasons. His word may be for you or someone else. He may testify to your spirit of God's faithfulness. He may give you direction. He may lead you to obey God's will for your life. He may speak into your spirit His special choice of companionship for marriage, ministry, or business. The Holy Ghost may be trying to close doors that are right but not timely for you. Finally, the Holy Ghost may speak a word of warning.

God is trying to intervene in your life. He may use you to intervene in the life of someone else who may not be answering His call. Whatever the case, you can be confident that it is right because our *Parakletos*, the Holy Ghost, only speaks the counsel that He has heard in Heaven.

Not for Prestige

A person who prays in tongues will not get the recognition and commendation of men. It is a very undesirable position. It is a very taxing, laborious position. You are working as hard as, if not harder than, the evangelist or pastor but don't receive the praise of men. No, this ministry, and it is a ministry, is obscured and isolated because it is seemingly insignificant.

It is a position that few have ever gotten to and even fewer remain in. Many walk around thrilled that they have the power of the Holy Ghost, but what are they doing with this anointing? God gives this power that we might function in its flow.

> *Allow the Holy Ghost to flow through you.*

One of the greatest blessings ever given to the church was the ability to talk to God on a higher level. God chose to do some of His most intimate communication from a mountain. God took Noah to Mt. Ararat, Abraham to Mt. Moriah, Moses to Mt. Horeb, Joshua to Hebron, Elijah to Mt. Carmel. Jesus told the apostle John to "come up hither" to receive the revelation.

In these last days God is calling together a Church that has gone beyond playing games. We have pushed our way into the holy of holies, and we're going to see a manifestation of God like never before in the history of the Church.

A secret code is being spoken from Heaven to earth and from earth to Heaven. Men and women will profit by receiving this secret code. As the Holy Ghost speaks through you, ask God to reveal His heart. You will begin to see God's guidance, direction, and comfort in new ways. This will profit you and others as you speak out what God has spoken into your spirit.

Thoughts and Reflections

_____

_____

_____

_____

_____

_____

_____

_____

_____

_____

_____

CHAPTER 5

THE INFLUENCE OF THE HOLY SPIRIT IN THE WORLD

The word *influence* may bring to mind something weird or strange. But the Holy Ghost is very influential in the world today. Influence means a "power that causes an effect by indirect or tangible ways." It means to alter drastically or to change the course of a thing. Jesus drastically influenced this world. After His ascension, He handed the baton to the Holy Ghost.

In the Old Testament, the Holy Spirit moved upon situations, people, or events and always changed them. He took an impossible situation and brought about remarkable change. When His mission was over, He returned to the One who sent Him.

The Holy Spirit often waited until the most critical moment before He showed up. This was divinely purposed so that no one or no thing would ever rob God of His glory. The Holy Spirit waited until He heard confessions like "It's too late," or "I can't," or "If God doesn't...." Then He stepped in and brought about a miracle.

Even though Jesus did tremendous works of power, He told His disciples that they would benefit more by His departure.

> *Nevertheless I tell you the truth; It is expedient for you that I go away: for if I go not away, the Comforter will not come unto you; but if I depart, I will send him unto you* (John 16:7).

Expedient means to be profitable, to be advantageous, to be necessary. Why would it be better for the Holy Ghost to come? Limited by an earthly body, Jesus could be in only one place at a time. Once the Holy Ghost was poured out, He could perform works of power wherever He found willing vessels.

The Holy Ghost is capable of changing any situation. Many people shun an anointed atmosphere because they know that it will challenge them to change. Preferring to stay where the power of God is not moving, they are never challenged, convicted, or transformed.

People do some things because they lack the presence of Jesus in their lives. If you knew that Jesus was right beside you, you would never do some of the things you do. The Holy Ghost makes you aware that He is watching your every move to deter you from evil.

> ## The Holy Ghost makes you aware of God's presence.

Orchestrating Change

It would be a sad day for the unsaved if the Holy Spirit stopped convicting men and drawing them to the Savior.

> *No man can come to me, except the Father which hath sent me draw him: and I will raise him up at the last day* (John 6:44).

The Holy Ghost is very instrumental in bringing salvation.

> *But when the Comforter is come, whom I will send unto you from the Father, even the Spirit of truth, which proceedeth from the Father, he shall testify of me* (John 15:26).

Let's look at His work in the world today:

> *And when he is come, he will reprove the world of sin, and of righteousness, and of judgment: of sin, because they believe not on me; of righteousness, because I go to my Father, and ye see me no more; of judgment,*

> *because the prince of this world is judged*
> (John 16:8-11).

According to this passage, the Holy Ghost has arrested you on three counts:

1. He has reproved your sin, which means to convict, to expose, to convince of a wrong, to tell a fault.

2. He convinces you of righteousness or a right standing with God. His goodness, not your own, saves you.

3. He will convince you of judgment, not only of your future encounter with God, but also of ungodly influences that cause you to sin.

The Holy Ghost wants to orchestrate change in your life. Many are pregnant with gifts and callings and miracles. Many are long overdue, and He is inducing labor to bring forth delivery. Because you have messed up, many of you believe your calling has been annulled. The devil is a liar, for *"the gifts and calling of God are without repentance"* (Rom. 11:29).

The Holy Ghost has come to convince and influence you to change. Dare to be different! Refuse to become a part of the mundane crowd going nowhere. Rise up and shake yourself. Find yourself a church that is reflecting change by the influence of the Holy Ghost.

Influence in Five Areas

1. *The Holy Ghost sets the stage for the Word of God.*

> *And the earth was without form, and void; and darkness was upon the face of the deep. And the Spirit of God moved upon the face of the waters* (Genesis 1:2).

Notice the condition of the earth: Without form means to lie in ruin, to be worthless, to be empty and in utter chaos. Void means to be empty, in an indistinguishable ruin. Darkness means more than the darkness we are familiar with. It means to bring misery and death.

When this world was in its utterly worthless, chaotic, miserable condition, the Spirit of God set the stage for a miracle. "*And the Spirit of God moved upon the face of the waters*" (Gen. 1:2).

Moved means to hover over, to bring warmth as a mother hen sits upon her nest. This warmth awakens the life inside the egg and stirs its desire to break forth. Life is present, but the shell must be broken. In the spirit realm we would call it a breakthrough.

The Spirit did the preparatory work. It was now up to the Word to give the command: "Let there be." The Word worked in conjunction with the Spirit. The Holy Spirit first moved, setting the stage for the command and authority of the Word.

The words "Let there be" imply that another force or influence was trying to prevent the transformation from chaos and confusion. Satan is the only other force or influence at work in this world system. He tries to prevent the work of God from coming into its fullness.

Praise Ushers in the Move of the Spirit

But thou art holy, O thou that inhabitest the praises of Israel (Psalm 22:3).

When praise goes up, the blessing comes down. Praise becomes the prerequisite to your miracle. Praise brings Jesus into your situation.

> *When praise goes up, blessing comes down.*

If you're facing a dilemma, praise Him. If you're in a valley, praise Him. If you're going through a storm, praise Him. As you praise Him, Jesus—the Living Word of God—will walk right into your dilemma and say, "Let it be so."

When Philip was preaching in Samaria, revival broke out (Acts 8:58).

And the angel of the Lord spake unto Philip, saying, Arise, and go toward the south unto

> *the way that goeth down from Jerusalem*
> *unto Gaza, which is desert* (Acts 8:26).
>
> *Then the Spirit said unto Philip, Go near,*
> *and join thyself to this chariot* (Acts 8:29).

An angel led Philip to an Ethiopian eunuch. Notice how the Holy Spirit set the stage, but then the Word took center stage. They both worked together to convert this influential man (Acts 8:30-38).

God promised the children of Israel that He would sustain them during their journey across the desert (Exod. 16:13-18). He sent them manna (a type of the Word). Before the manna came, however, the ground would be covered with dew (a type of the Holy Spirit, the breathing presence of God). Once again the Holy Spirit set the stage for the Word.

2. The Holy Spirit's influence will separate and declare.

He separated light from darkness, declared what they would be, and placed them in order (Gen. 1:4-5). He then separated the firmament and divided the waters. He called the firmament Heaven (Gen. 1:6-8). He then separated the water from the dry land and declared the dry land to be earth; the waters He named seas (Gen. 1:9-10).

The Holy Spirit will do the same thing in our lives. He will separate certain things from you, set limitations, and declare your destiny. God separated the children of Israel from Egypt. He set borders for them and went before them to drive out their enemies, but they had to go in and possess the Promised Land. God said:

> *Every place whereon the soles of your feet shall tread shall be yours: from the wilderness and Lebanon, from the river, the river Euphrates, even unto the uttermost sea shall your coast be* (Deuteronomy 11:24).

The Holy Spirit is separating you that He might declare on earth what Heaven has known from eternity.

3. *The Holy Spirit wants to resurrect buried seeds in your life (Gen. 1:11-12).*

The seeds were there, but they were obscured. God brought forth creatures from the waters (Gen. 1:20). They were there, but the Word brought them forth from what had covered them. God commanded the earth to bring forth living creatures (Gen. 1:24). They were there, but simply had to be brought forth.

God formed man from dust. But man, like anything else, is merely a form of what he can be before the Holy Spirit breathes into him vibrancy and freshness of life. Only then does the form become a living being.

God Mines for Gold

Job endured tremendous emotional pain and physical affliction. His troubles were not only known to God but were allowed by God. Losing his sons and daughters and possessions left Job feeling very much alone. He looked at his situation from every possible angle, trying to find God.

Job finally concluded:

> *But he knoweth the way that I take: when he hath tried me, I shall come forth as gold* (Job 23:10).

Until then, he would not curse God and die.

Every gold mine is hidden beneath the earth. Mining priceless jewels takes many hours of painstaking labor. Tons of earth must be removed to find the gold.

In the same way, a gold mine is buried beneath your flesh. Crucifying your flesh is excruciating, but it must occur to reveal the priceless jewels within you. Give God digging rights. After all, the mine belongs to Him. Allow Him to dig deep and bring out buried treasure.

> *Allow God to expose your buried treasure.*

The devil knows you're a gold mine waiting to be claimed and mined. Your adversary has covered your priceless jewels with your past, unconfessed sins, emotional traumas, and religious tradition. Little does the devil know that you have been buried alive. You merely need the Spirit to move, and the Word uncovers you. You are Heaven's best kept secret and hell's worst nightmare.

4. *The Holy Spirit wrestles with us to bring us to a deeper commitment.*

> *And the Lord said, My spirit shall not always strive with man, for that he also is flesh: yet his days shall be an hundred and twenty years* (Genesis 6:3).

If we could only see the different spirits and attitudes that we deal with in people. Have you ever wondered why you feel so spent and drained after ministry? Is it because of physical exertion? Partly. The majority of the battle comes from contending with opposing forces. This is why prayer is so important to any ministry.

We need the Holy Spirit to go before us, preparing people's hearts and minds for the Word. If the Holy Ghost truly comes upon you, He will change your life. You might not dance, you might not speak in tongues, but in some way you will be changed.

In these last days, we are not going to be dealing with novices from the kingdom of darkness. Generals and colonels from the pit of the damned will try to assault the Church. As the Holy Spirit brings us to full submission, another influence opposes Him.

We Choose Who Wins

I read an article once about a man who had two dogs. Every weekend the owner let the dogs fight and placed bets on who would win. After several weekends a man noticed the owner never lost a bet. He approached the owner, questioning him as to the secret of his success.

"It's very simple," replied the man. "It's my choice. If I want the one dog to win, I starve the other one."

This is true in the spirit realm. The Holy Spirit is there to wrestle and help us decide to feed our spirit man while starving the flesh. The stronger one will win.

As the Holy Spirit wrestles with us, another influence is always present:

> *I find then a law, that, when I would do good, evil is present with me. For I delight in the law of God after the inward man: but I see another law in my members, warring against the law of my mind, and bringing me into captivity to the law of sin which is in my members* (Romans 7:21-23).

> *Now there was a day when the sons of God came to present themselves before the Lord, and Satan came also among them* (Job 1:6).

The spirit of lawlessness always tries to lead us away from where the Holy Spirit wants to take us. If we heed this second force, he will bring us into captivity. As we present ourselves to God, satan and his evil influence oppose, tempt, and accuse us. We choose who wins.

When Winning Is Losing

As the Holy Spirit strives with you to bring you into submission and obedience, you may be holding on to the very thing that He wants. As you walk away you may feel as though you've won, but you've actually lost.

Some of you are headed down rapids that will twist and turn you upside down and inside out. If you are persistent in your ways, God will stand by watching the fight that you think you won, but in all reality you lost.

Some of you have matured, and the Holy Spirit wants to take you higher. But it's a choice.

> *Therefore leaving the principles of the doctrine of Christ, let us go on unto perfection; not laying again the foundation of repentance from dead works, and of faith toward God, of the doctrine of baptisms, and of laying on of hands, and of resurrection of the dead, and of eternal judgment. And this will we do, if God permit* (Hebrews 6:1-3).

We find the same words in Genesis chapter 1. *"Let us...."* God asks you to push away from the familiar into the supernatural. People resist change, but in order to get to where God wants us—and to arrive on time—you must push away.

God wanted to bring Israel into the Promised Land, a land full of milk and honey. Milk denotes sustenance; honey denotes sweetness of victory. But it was a choice.

Noah had a choice. God said, *"Come thou..."* (Gen. 7:1). He had to answer the call. Even after he got on board, he had a choice. The ark had three levels. Level one, where he first got on board, felt the turbulence from the waves. On level three Noah rode on top of the waters and could look out a window that gave him access to God. The view was not available on level one.

5. *The Holy Spirit seeks a place to rest in authority (Gen. 8:8-12).*

The dove symbolizes the Holy Spirit (Matt. 3:16-17). A dove flies up to 150 miles to find good migration. A dove makes its nest far above the earth, usually perched in a cleft of a rock. A dove fights for supremacy in the nest. They resist with fierce, decisive measures every species that tries to dwell in their home.

What can we conclude from this analogy?

- The Holy Spirit seeks to find migration in your life.

- The Holy Spirit will cause you to build your nest in a rock. David said:

From the end of the earth will I cry unto thee, when my heart is overwhelmed: lead me to the rock that is higher than I (Psalm 61:2).

We can attain a place in God that is higher than our problems, giving us a divine perspective. We must be led to this place. It is against our nature to want this rock. We must oppose our flesh and say, "When my spirit is overwhelmed, my spirit goes beyond nature and finds satisfaction only in the supernatural." We ask God to do something our flesh does not want: to lead us to the rock—Jesus—and away from earthly logic.

- The Holy Spirit will fight for you. He will go to war for you as strange birds seek to enter your nest.

- The Holy Spirit seeks rest for the sole of His foot (Gen. 8:8-12). While the raven (our old nature) finds rest in an earth under judgment, the dove takes a different approach. He flew around and searched but found no place to rest. God wants to find a resting place for His authority:

Thus saith the Lord, The heaven is my throne, and the earth is my footstool: where is the house that ye build unto me? and where is the place of my rest? (Isaiah 66:1).

Nor by the earth; for it is his footstool: neither by Jerusalem; for it is the city of the great King (Matthew 5:35).

The Holy Spirit flew on missions in the Old Testament as He rested upon Abraham, Isaac, and Jacob, but they were not the one. He flew upon Moses, enabling him to lead the exodus. He flew upon Samson and found periodic rest, but it was short-lived as he slept in the lap of Delilah.

He flew upon David, saying, "Surely this is the Lord's anointed," but he became an adulterer and murderer. He loved him, but he was not the one. He flew upon Daniel, but he was not the one. He lighted upon Isaiah, but he was not the one. The prophet wrote about another one coming:

> *For unto us a child is born, unto us a son is given: and the government shall be upon his shoulder: and his name shall be called Wonderful, Counsellor, The mighty God, The everlasting Father, The Prince of Peace. Of the increase of his government and peace there shall be no end, upon the throne of David, and upon his kingdom, to order it, and to establish it with judgment and with justice from henceforth even for ever. The zeal of the Lord of hosts will perform this* (Isaiah 9:6-7).

He flew upon Jeremiah, but the weeping prophet wasn't the one. He then rested upon Ezekiel and performed many mighty deeds, but Ezekiel was not the one.

Finally, He looked from the portals of glory and saw the One. There was only One found worthy in Heaven and earth for the dove to land upon.

As Jesus stood in the Jordan, the dove descended from Heaven, saying, "I have found him whom my soul loveth." He landed upon Him, and His authority and anointing rested upon Jesus. The Holy Ghost found a body to land upon and to inhabit with authority.

Jesus died, but He said, *"Father, into thy hands I commend* [put into your trust] *my spirit"* (Luke 23:46). This same dove swept down from glory as a mighty rushing wind (Acts 2:2). He found a body, the Church, to inhabit and to rest His authority upon.

Will You Clear the Runway!

As I flew into JFK Airport one day, I noticed that our pilot was circling for a long time. He announced that fog had obscured the runway and he would continue to circle until the fog dissipated. After quite some time in the air, we finally were cleared to land.

In a spiritual sense, the runway was me; the jetliner was a type of the dove, the Holy Spirit. The Holy Spirit wants desperately to land. He desires to touch down upon the children of God, but we must clear ourselves and give Him permission to land. As the Holy Spirit circles, He sees some things that must be cleared from our lives before He lands.

Make room for the Holy Spirit. He wants to settle on your wounds, your past, your trauma, even your greatest weakness. But you are the key. Will you clear the runway? If not, He will circle for a while, but then He will seek another runway.

Give the Holy Ghost permission to land on your life. You'll never be the same.

Thoughts and Reflections

CHAPTER 6

THE CRY OF A BARREN WOMB

Israelite women often wept bitterly as a result of their barrenness. Jewish women took to heart the covenant between God and Abraham that promised to bless and multiply the seed that would ultimately bring forth the Christ child. Barren women like Rachel cried out:

> *And when Rachel saw that she bare Jacob no children, Rachel envied her sister; and said unto Jacob, Give me children, or else I die* (Genesis 30:1).

God wants His bride, the Church, to bring forth fruit to His glory. How do we do that? Jesus said:

> *I am the vine, ye are the branches: He that abideth in me* [remains in constant

fellowship], *and I in him, the same bringeth forth much fruit: for without me ye can do nothing* (John 15:5).

As we bear fruit, God will purge us that we might bring forth more fruit:

> *Every branch in me that beareth not fruit he taketh away: and every branch that beareth fruit, he purgeth it, that it may bring forth more fruit* (John 15:2).

As we continue to walk in obedience, we produce much fruit. Why should we bear fruit?

> *Herein is my Father glorified, that ye bear much fruit; so shall ye be my disciples* (John 15:8).

But we also benefit.

> *These things have I spoken unto you, that my joy might remain in you, and that your joy might be full* (John 15:11).

We live in a despondent, depraved, and defeated society. The very thing that this world needs should be hanging on the limbs of the Church. They need love, joy, peace—the fruit of the Spirit. As the Holy Ghost saturates and fills our lives, we produce fruit. This is God's way of meeting the needs of lost humanity.

The fruit of the righteous is a tree of life; and he that winneth souls is wise (Proverbs 11:30).

Jesus told a parable about a man who found no fruit on his fig tree. Grieved at its lack of productivity, the owner wanted to cut it down. But the vinedresser asked to cultivate it one more year. If it didn't produce fruit, it would be cut down (Luke 13:6-9).

Fruit bearing is a serious thing with Jesus. The cry of the Church should be, "Give us children, lest we die!"

Never Satisfied

Solomon mentions four things that are never satisfied:

The horseleach hath two daughters, crying, Give, give. There are three things that are never satisfied, yea, four things say not, It is enough: The grave; and the barren womb; the earth that is not filled with water; and the fire that saith not, It is enough (Proverbs 30:15-16).

Several married couples in Scripture had intimate relations and yet lacked children: Abraham and Sarah, Isaac and Rebekah, Jacob and Rachel. These wives cried out because of a barren womb.

The same thing happens today when we merely go to church but lack intimacy with the Holy Ghost. The womb of our soul becomes barren. We need to cry out and not be satisfied until we become impregnated with the fruit of the Holy Spirit.

Do You Want Children?

Many are afraid to fall in love with the Holy Ghost because they know that commitment brings intimacy, and intimacy brings conception, and conception brings labor, and labor produces a baby. As in the natural realm, it takes an intimate relationship to conceive.

Many Christians have spiritual orgasms but never conceive a child. Many do not want children because they do not want commitment and responsibility. They do not want to endure nine months of carrying the child. Many have been impregnated by the Holy Ghost but have chosen to abort the baby. Other Christians who cannot carry their baby to term have miscarried.

The womb was designed as a receptacle for the seed of man and a place for a conceived child to develop. God gave Eve the responsibility, and the blessing, of bringing forth children (Gen. 3:16). The Bible says Adam knew his wife (Gen. 4:1,25). This intimate relationship gave them a son. You can trace the lineage of Christ back to the fruit of this first intimate relationship.

Mary was a virgin when the angel announced she would have a baby. She asked, *"How shall this be, seeing I know not a man?"* (Luke 1:34). This child was conceived by the power of the Holy Ghost.

The angel told her:

> *The Holy Ghost shall come upon thee, and the power of the Highest shall overshadow thee: therefore also that holy thing which shall be born of thee shall be called the Son of God* (Luke 1:35).

Three things were to happen:

1. Conception: *"Thou shalt conceive"* (Luke 1:31).
2. Intimacy: *"The Holy Ghost shall come upon thee."*
3. Implanting of the Seed: *"The power of the Highest shall overshadow thee."*

It was totally the work of the Holy Ghost, but He had to have a womb in which to do His work.

Who Are You Inwardly?

Man is made in God's image and likeness. We are also a triune being—body, soul, and spirit. God has saved our spirits. Our bodies are not saved. The body does not want to be holy or bring forth good fruit. Your body will never wake you up at 3:00 a.m. and tell you to pray. The body will never encourage you to live right. The body will never restrain you from gossiping. The body is flesh and will always be flesh.

David prayed:

Search me, O God, and know my heart: try me, and know my thoughts (Psalm 139:23).

What does God use to search us?

The spirit of man is the candle of the Lord, searching all the inward parts of the belly (Proverbs 20:27).

This verse shows us three truths:

1. Man is not only body and soul, but also spirit.

2. The spirit of man is the candle of the Lord.

3. The Lord uses this spirit to search the innermost being of man.

Underneath your shout, your dance, your speaking in tongues, who are you really? This has always been the problem with manmade holiness. Trying to change a person outwardly only leaves him or her frustrated, confused, and feeling like a failure.

God does just the opposite. He changes you from the inside out. Out of the abundance of the heart the mouth speaks. Changing from the outside in has no lasting effect. It always leaves the womb barren, crying, "It's not enough!" Changing from the outside in is like painting a building without removing the trash that clutters the inside.

There is a difference between repainting and repenting. Repainting changes the outside, repenting changes the inside.

Our Spirits Are Joined

The Spirit itself beareth witness with our spirit, that we are the children of God (Romans 8:16).

This Scripture deals with two spirits—the spirit of man and the Holy Spirit. Joined together at salvation, the Holy Spirit testifies to our spirit that we are saved.

One of the greatest blessings is that His work is invisible. He can testify in your spirit when all hell is breaking loose, and no one would know it but you.

He speaks to the very areas that you have tried to change without success. You may be tearful over these areas. You may have buried areas of your life over the years, trying to dispose of them. Something just won't let you throw them away.

Have you ever wanted something and knew it was God's will, but you just couldn't seem to get a breakthrough? As you see someone with the very thing you want, it causes a kicking inside you. This lets you know that your baby is still there. You haven't aborted or miscarried. As you walk the floor at night, the Holy Spirit lets you know it's still in you.

What happens next is simply awesome. The Holy Spirit becomes so much of a part of your life that you begin to have more than just a Sunday morning fling with Him. You begin to know the Holy Spirit and understand His purpose. You become sensitive to His feelings, which keeps you from grieving the Holy Spirit. You begin to feel a burning love and appreciation for the Holy Spirit, which helps you to obey and submit to His leading. This keeps the flame of spiritual passion burning in your spirit.

As a result of your daily communion with the Holy Spirit, the barren areas in your life that have cried out for years—the spiritual womb that has never been satisfied—now becomes impregnated by the Holy Spirit.

A Deepening Relationship

A man and a woman who like each other become friends and get to know each other. As they sense a growing attachment for one another, they decide to date. As their commitment grows, they advance to a deeper level of relationship. Eventually, they become engaged. A ring signifies the bond between them. One day they stand before witnesses and enter into marriage. This causes them to share themselves in a more intimate way. Their new physical intimacy brings about conception and ultimately birth.

Deepen your relationship with God through intimacy.

As the Spirit of God bears witness with our spirit, we deepen our relationship with God.

> *Deep calleth unto deep at the noise of thy waterspouts: all thy waves and thy billows are gone over me* (Psalm 42:7).

God wants the Church to go beyond a surface relationship where He is just a friend.

He calls us to go steady; He then wants an engagement; ultimately, He wants an intimate relationship that joins the Holy Spirit together with our spirit. Cultivating intimacy eventually results in conception and birth. Your barren womb is no more.

Present at Birth, Manifested in Maturity

The parents each contribute a gene to their child. One gene is usually dominant. In the spirit realm this is also true.

Certain traits are manifested in the child from each parent. The child may have physical characteristics like one of his parents: eyes, nose, hands, feet, hair color, etc. Other traits, however, will only be known in time and with maturity.

The traits of our parents' genes are within us. Just as in the original creation, the seeds were in the ground but were locked up. The Holy Ghost worked in conjunction with the Word to bring about a release. This is why God said, "Let there be," meaning let it come forth.

God commanded Adam to know his wife and multiply. Likewise, as the Church has an intimate relationship with the Holy Ghost, we will begin to produce spiritual offspring or the fruit of the Spirit.

The angel who told Mary that she would be the mother of Jesus also listed the characteristics of the holy offspring (Luke 1:32-33):

1. He shall be great.
2. He shall be the Son or offspring of the Highest.
3. He shall be given the throne of His father David, which denotes authority.
4. He shall reign, which denotes lordship.

The Church is the bride of Christ. We are espoused as *"a chaste virgin to Christ"* (2 Cor. 11:2). We are to supply our spiritual womb to the Holy Ghost. As a result of our relationship, our barren womb which is crying, dissatisfied, and longing for intimacy and fulfillment with Jesus will begin to produce offspring in His likeness. Some of His traits will be obvious from the very outset, while others will need maturity and commitment to come to full fruition.

Producing Something Holy

When Jesus Christ was born of a virgin, people didn't know how to react. Shepherds heard the angels sing, "Glory to God in the highest!" They came and saw Him wrapped in swaddling clothes in a manger.

Simeon held Jesus in the temple and declared Him to be the consolation of Israel. Herod tried to kill Him. Many believed Jesus was a mere human. After hearing Him speak, however, they knew He was more than flesh.

Even though you live in a fleshly body, the Holy Ghost wants to birth in you a holy thing—an experience that goes beyond logic, human love, and mere spiritual excitement that leaves you turned on but empty. The Holy Ghost wants to impregnate you with a seed that will produce something holy in you.

> *Produce something holy through the Holy Ghost.*

As long as you merely have a fling with the Holy Ghost, your womb will remain empty. If, after you have reached your climax and had your spiritual orgasm, your womb still is barren and crying out, then you have missed your purpose on earth.

It's an honor to carry something for Jesus and bring it to birth. It's an honor to look at your spiritual offspring and say, "This is born of God!" Whatever God births in you—a ministry, a book, a song, a message—you know whatever is born of God overcomes the world. This spiritual offspring has all the characteristics of its heavenly Father.

What's the Difference?

You can never look at a Spirit-filled child of God and say that their fruit is the Holy Spirit. It isn't the Holy Spirit; it is merely the offspring or production of the Holy Spirit.

Fruit is something that takes time to be developed. It's just like a husband and wife who share a physical intimacy. Even though the woman conceives seed, it still takes nine months for the baby to be born. When the mother delivers the child, you merely see the end result of a nine-month progressive work.

Here's my point: The baby is not the father, but he is the result of the seed of his father. He did not precede the father; the father preceded him. The baby did not produce the father; the father produced the baby.

The wife supplied the womb; the father supplied the seed; intimacy brought about conception. The child resembles its father. It has his blood, his eyes, his characteristics, and his features.

Likewise, the Church is the bride of Christ. We supply the womb; the Holy Ghost supplies the seed; our relationship with God brings about conception. As we bring forth spiritual offspring, they should resemble the Father.

Fruit—Not Fruits—of the Spirit

> *But the fruit of the Spirit is love, joy, peace, longsuffering, gentleness, goodness, faith, meekness, temperance: against such there is no law* (Galatians 5:22-23).

The term "fruits of the Spirit" is not a scriptural term. The nine functions of the Holy Spirit mentioned in Galatians 5:22-23 do not come from nine different spirits; they are the result of one Spirit.

An orange has many sections, but it is one orange that resulted from one seed. An ear of corn has hundreds of kernels that resulted from one kernel. The ground conceived the grain and a few months later brought forth a finished product. A baby has one body but many functions that resulted from his mother conceiving the father's seed and allowing him to develop for nine months.

The apostle Paul tells us that the nine fu nctions, traits, or characteristics are the result of one Spirit. He calls this the *"fruit of the Spirit"* (Gal. 5:22).

No Limits!

After giving his discourse on the nine fruit of the one Spirit, the apostle Paul makes a very intriguing statement. He says, *"Against such there is no law"* (Gal. 5:23).

We have laws that define right and wrong. They also govern, regulate, or set limits on our behavior. If these limits are exceeded, you have broken the law. For example, you can drive only 65 miles per hour on interstates in West Virginia. If this is exceeded, you have broken the law.

With this thought in mind, Paul tells us to put the pedal to the metal in regard to the fruit of the Spirit. There is no law to govern how much of these Father-like traits you can have as a child of God. Unlimited love, joy, and peace are available to you.

You Hold the Key

Do you know that no one, not even the devil, can keep you from acting like your Father in Heaven? We need to be keenly aware of the feelings of the Holy Spirit. While there are no limits on how much you look and act like your Father, we can hinder the Holy Spirit in several ways:

1. We can fail to spend intimate times alone with the Holy Spirit, resulting in our never really knowing Him. It would be like being married to a total stranger. Although you may cohabit the same house, no communication or sharing occurs.

2. We can grieve the Holy Spirit (Eph. 4:30), which means to insult, to hurt the feeling of, or to make one sad.

3. We can quench the Holy Spirit (1 Thess. 5:19), which means to extinguish much like you would a fire.

4. We can lie to the Holy Ghost (Acts 5:3). The Bible says that satan filled their hearts. The word *filled* means to cram full.

5. We can tempt the Spirit (Acts 5:9).

We should avoid these at all costs. God forbid that we would have at our disposal the awesome power of the Holy Ghost and not seize Him. He wants to bring us into an intimate relationship with Jesus Christ that will cause us to become impregnated with destiny.

The Holy Ghost wants us to know God as Adam knew (to have closeness or intimacy with) Eve (Gen. 4:1,25). Then we will produce the promised seed and begin to bear the fruit of the Spirit. Only when Adam knew Eve intimately did he produce offspring.

Thermometer or Thermostat?

The Holy Ghost functions like a thermostat and a thermometer. The thermometer reflects its surrounding temperature, and the thermostat controls the inside heating system that gives the thermometer its reading.

What is your thermometer reading?

In the same way, the Holy Ghost works inside you. Your outward actions (what you say and do) reflect your temperature to those around you. Let's look at the outward manifestation of a Spirit-filled life:

> But the fruit of the Spirit is love, joy, peace, longsuffering, gentleness, goodness, faith, meekness, temperance: against such there is no law (Galatians 5:22-23).

This passage describes three sets of triplets. We will break these down and give each set a categorical name.

1. Atmosphere

2. Attitude

3. Attribute

The atmosphere is your surroundings. You may find yourself in a very hostile atmosphere where the fruit and works of the flesh are being manifested. As you yield to the Holy Spirit, however, He will throw a wet blanket on the unkind thing that you wanted to say.

The Holy Spirit will build a fire of His own that will bring warmth to a cold atmosphere, hope to a despairing atmosphere, joy to a saddening atmosphere, and love to a bitter, revengeful atmosphere. This is why the first three triplets—love, joy, and peace—are atmosphere-changing fruit.

The second three triplets—longsuffering, gentleness, goodness—are attitude-changing fruit. Even though we are saved and filled with the Holy Ghost, each of us has the potential to have an attitude. God sometimes lets us go through difficult situations to let us see what's really inside us. When we see our own helplessness, weaknesses, and despair, it causes us to cry out, "God, I need You!"

You may have been good to someone who later used you. You may have gone the extra mile for someone who betrayed you. You may have dealt with someone in gentleness who turned on you and abused you.

God works even in these hardships. As you cry out, God will take your inability to do what you know is right and make it a platform for His opportunity. You can bear longsuffering, gentleness, and goodness.

An attribute is simply a personality or character trait. If left to our own devices, we would make the same conclusion as the apostle Paul: "*Wretched man that I am!*" (Rom. 7:24). We may know what is right and want to do it, but we don't know how (See Rom. 7:15-25).

God does His most excellent work when the odds are against Him. He waits until the boat is full of water before He walks on top of your storm. He waits until the furnace of your trial is seven times hotter than normal to show Himself as the fourth man. He waits until Lazarus is decomposing to resurrect him. He waits until three doctors have agreed that you have an inoperable tumor before He steps in.

He will step in.

You have a strength that defies human logic. You have an ability to stand that you cannot attribute to anyone but God. You have a peace that even the apostle Paul couldn't understand, so he called it the *"peace of God, which passeth all understanding"* (Phil. 4:7). You have a joy that the apostle Peter could not describe, so he called it *"joy unspeakable and full of glory"* (1 Pet. 1:8).

We call this third triplet—faith, meekness, and self-control—attribute because these qualities cannot be attributed to you but only to the Holy Ghost.

Within you lies the ability to become whatever you choose to be. Remember that you have a choice, and the choice does not come without a price.

Fruit Is Born Out of Death

Truth can be seen in the physical and spiritual realms. Jesus illustrated a dynamic spiritual truth with a common example:

> *Verily, verily, I say unto you, Except a corn of wheat fall into the ground and die, it abideth alone: but if it die, it bringeth forth much fruit* (John 12:24).

After a seed is dropped into the ground, its shell must die, decompose, or pass away. This outer casing has only one purpose: to house the heart of the grain, which produces new life.

This outer casing is like our flesh, which houses our soul and spirit. As we crucify the flesh (Gal. 5:24) and *"seek those things which are above"* (Col. 3:1), the life of the Spirit comes to full fruition in us.

Then we can say confidently:

> *I am crucified with Christ: nevertheless I live; yet not I, but Christ liveth in me: and the life which I now live in the flesh I live by the faith of the Son of God, who loved me, and gave himself for me* (Galatians 2:20).

You Must Wait Patiently

When a seed is dropped into the ground and covered, it lies dormant for a season. No one can see it; no one can tell that anything is happening. But during this time the process of germination takes place. The casing is dying, the heart of grain is sprouting.

In the spiritual realm it is no different. The apostle Paul tells the Colossians:

> *Mortify therefore your members which are upon the earth; fornication, uncleanness, inordinate affection, evil concupiscence, and covetousness, which is idolatry* (Colossians 3:5).

Mortify is a term related to mortuary, a place where we find nothing but dead and dysfunctional bodies.

What is Paul saying? Stop your Adamic nature from being the dominant force in your life. Allow the Holy Ghost to work in you, putting to death the flesh so that new life may sprout from you.

Put the flesh to death.

The same principle is found in Numbers 17:1-8, where God took something seemingly dead (Aaron's rod) and caused it to bud. You may long to function and produce. If you feel barren, you know how the Jewish wives wept because of their barren wombs.

It is time for the Church, which is the bride of Christ, to weep because of our barrenness.

Within every one of you is a spirit that cries out as Jacob, "I knowI am Jacob now, but within me is the desire to become Israel!"

Whose Baby Are You Carrying?

Let me close this chapter with a question: Whose baby are you carrying? In the middle of the night you feel it kicking. Some of you are long overdue, but you just felt destiny kicking to let you know satan has not aborted your baby.

Old farmers say that finding a spot of blood in the egg tells you that the rooster had been with the hen. Within your spirit is a womb that is with child of the Holy Ghost. Mary supplied the womb; the Holy Ghost supplied the seed; and the seed supplied the blood.

Every child can be traced back to its father by its DNA. Your blood type is 100 percent a result of the seed of your father. It is just normal that you begin to take on some of the character traits of your father. You may have his eyes, his hair, his nose. Someone may say you act just like your dad.

May that be said of us after we realize that we are carrying the baby of the Holy Ghost. May we cry out against mediocrity, compromise, and a spirit of indifference that only lead to a barren, unsatisfied womb.

Thoughts and Reflections

REVIVING
WHAT REMAINS

The word *revelation* means to uncover a thing, to reveal, to fully disclose a matter. Revelation is an act of God that is just as real as God Himself. It is a divine blessing for an all-wise, all-knowing God to uncover a matter, to reveal His will, and to manifest His plans for your life.

Revelation from God comes in three segments: past, present, and future. First, God sometimes reveals things in our past for instruction or edification. Jesus told the apostle John on the isle of Patmos, "*Write the things which thou hast seen* [past], *and the things which are* [present]" (Rev. 1:19). Sometimes God reaches into your storm or dilemma and tells you everything will be all right. *"Write...the things which shall be hereafter* [future]" (Rev. 1:19).

Come Up Higher

The apostle John recorded these words:

> *After this I looked, and, behold, a door was opened in heaven: and the first voice which I heard was as it were of a trumpet talking with me; which said, Come up hither, and I will shew thee things which must be hereafter* (Revelation 4:1).

The primary context of this verse and its primary doctrinal interpretation is thought to be the rapture of the Church. But every primary interpretation has a secondary application. God ushered the apostle Paul up to the third heaven to receive tremendous revelation (2 Cor. 12:1-5).

Revelation Comes From the Spirit

Jesus declared the same thing to all seven churches in Revelation chapters 2 and 3:

> *He that hath an ear, let him hear what the Spirit saith unto the churches* (Revelation 3:6).

First Corinthians 2:9-14 gives us some more insight into this verse. What the Spirit reveals is totally awesome. The scope of God's blessing covers what eye has not seen and what ear has not heard. It gets even more mind-blowing than that! The storehouse of God's will for our lives includes blessings that we have never even thought about—things that surpass even our wildest imaginations; things that have never even entered our hearts. That's awesome!

> *But God hath revealed them unto us by his Spirit: for the Spirit searcheth all things, yea, the deep things of God* (1 Corinthians 2:10).

The apostle Paul calls them *"the deep things of God."* Many of us never get past the first oracles or the starting place with God.

The storehouse of Heaven is full. You will never exhaust its inventory of glory. If we aren't walking in such a way to access it, however, these glorious realities will never occur in our lives.

> ***You have access to Heaven's full storehouse.***

> *Therefore leaving the principles of the doctrine of Christ, let us go on unto perfection...* (Hebrews 6:1).

This Scripture signifies that we must move away from where we first started with God.

Noah's ark was constructed with a first, second, and third floor. But the window, which gave Noah access to Heaven, was placed on the third floor. If Noah stayed on the first or second floor, he could not see out the window. We must get in a position to see.

Many Christians never access the windows of Heaven because they are still living in the outer court and have never broken through to the third dimension, the holy of holies. Many live in defeat and carnality because they have remained on the same level where they first boarded the ark of salvation.

Once there was a little boy who kept falling out of bed. His mother securely tucked him in only to hear the thump on the floor as he fell out once again. After the third time she decided to stay at the door and see why he was falling out. She noticed the boy slept close to the edge where he first climbed in. One wrong turn caused him to fall out.

Many fall out of fellowship with God because they never move up to the third floor. This is why they feel the turbulence of the waves in every storm. They have stayed too close to where they first got in.

Don't Digress!

The seven churches discussed in Revelation represent seven ages of time beginning at approximately A.D. 96 and running to the present.

More importantly, however, these seven churches represent seven stages of the church age.

In Revelation 2:1, Jesus walked in the midst of the church at Ephesus. In Revelation 3:20, He stands on the outside knocking for an entrance. This shows the digression of the church. Each one of these churches depicts our life as a child of God at one time or another.

1. We have left our first love (Rev. 2:4).

2. We have been crushed as the church of Smyrna, a city noted for its perfume or myrrh (Rev. 2:8).

3. We have had the spirit of Pergamos in us, which has caused others to stumble (Rev. 2:14).

4. We have things in us that were strong but now have begun to die as is the case with the church of Sardis (Rev. 3:2).

This revelation came as a result of the seven spirits of God and seven stars. The seven spirits denote perfection or completion. It is not seven different spirits, but shows the fullness of one Spirit (Isa. 11:2). The seven stars denote the ministers. The word they preached, in conjunction with the Spirit, brought about this revelation to the churches (Rev. 1:20).

Let's look at the messages in Revelation chapters 2 and 3:

1. God says to the churches, "I know." These are humbling—even frightening —words. Just think of all there is to know about you. God says, "I know."

2. God says, "I know thy works." God looks beyond surface appearance and says, "I know what others do not know because I know the heart."

3. God says, "I know your name." God knows our name or reputation. God says, "Yes, I have heard the gossip. I have heard what kind of reputation you have." Did you know that God knows your name and still loves you? He can know your reputation and still use you. He can know who you really are behind that worship, behind that song, behind that dance, behind your tongues, behind your preaching.

He knows who you really are.

God says, "I know the truth. I know your name." God knows that your name is Jacob but still asks, "What is thy name?" Anytime an all-wise, all-knowing God asks a question, it isn't for His benefit. You need to confess,

"My name is Jacob." Even though He knows our name, He wants us to confess it because He is going to change our name and speak a glorious destiny over us.

My sheep hear my voice, and I know them, and they follow me (John 10:27).

Jesus knows His sheep by name, and He cares for and loves each one of them.

And unto the angel of the church in Sardis write; These things saith he that hath the seven Spirits of God, and the seven stars; I know thy works, that thou hast a name that thou livest, and art dead. Be watchful, and strengthen the things which remain, that are ready to die: for I have not found thy works perfect before God (Revelation 3:1-2).

4. God sees beyond the name to the reality. Death means a separation, to cut off. It's like turning a light switch to the off position, which breaks the circuit and cuts off the power. God says, "I know that you are separated from life. Your name may say differently, but I know."

5. God also reveals a blessing. Something remained to work with. Jesus said three things in Rev. 3:2:

- *"Be watchful."* The word *watchful* means to awaken or arouse something that is at the point of dying. It isn't dead yet. If the Holy Spirit said these things which remained were ready to die, there was still a little life left.

- Maybe you have felt that your ministry is dead. If you feel any kick at all, you need to be aroused and to awaken because the movement tells you it's still alive.

- *"Strengthen the things that remain."* The word *strengthen* means to solidify, to establish, to set upright again; to take something that has been weakened and build it back up.

Within you are gifts, callings, and talents that have been weakened, pressed down, or held back. Your vision, dream, or desire may have been crushed. You may not have had any control over the circumstances. Perhaps your disobedience grieved the Holy Spirit. But arise, my friend! Whatever the devil did to you, he didn't complete the job. He left some strength in you.

- The apostle Paul said:

Most gladly therefore will I rather glory in my infirmities, that the power of Christ may rest upon me (2 Corinthians 12:9).

- When his strength had given out and his resources were exhausted, he had no other place to turn. He could rely on no other strength but the strength that God gave him.

- Your own strength is not enough, but if you will take what's left of it and give it to God, who is more than enough, you will find Him to be sufficient.

- Nehemiah looked at the ruined walls of Jerusalem and wept. He took the little bit that the devil had left and rebuilt the wall. Some of you are weeping over what the enemy has stolen from you. As you weep your way into depression and anxiety, the enemy causes you to lose focus on what is left.

- Arise, my friend, and seize what is left. So what if your joy isn't what it used to be? Use what is left. So what if your desire is dampened? Take hold of what is left. So what if your power is almost gone? Seize what is left and be what God said you could be. Don't let circumstances abort your dream.

> ## *Don't let circumstances abort your dream.*

- *"That are ready to die."* If a person is ready to die, we don't necessarily make funeral arrangements. We care for and nourish the little life that remains. Sometimes we have to put them in ICU, but we don't give up. Sometimes we do extensive surgery, but we don't give up. Sometimes we put them on life support. A machine may assist them in breathing, but we don't give up until they are stable enough to breathe on their own.

Satan would love to see you say the last rites over your ministry. If you feel near death spiritually, don't major on the fact that you are dying; major on the fact that you are half alive.

In the Parable of the Good Samaritan, Jesus said the thieves left the man *"half dead"* (Luke 10:30). His enemies made a big mistake. They left the man with just enough life to revive. He came back to life.

Some of you may have been diagnosed with a terminal illness. Place your case in the hands of the Great Physician. Refuse to accept the verdict. Get a second opinion.

It's Time to Take Inventory

Your miracle is not in what you lost. Your miracle is in what is left. God is not discouraged by your lack. He encourages you to rise and seize what is left.

God knows, which tells me He is not surprised. These two words may seem insignificant, but they are crucial for us to understand. You don't have to pretend. God knows everything isn't all right. God knows you aren't on top of the situation. God knows you are a 911 case. God knows you are in critical condition. In spite of your dilemma, He says, "It's not over until I say it's over."

In the midst of your trial, dilemma, or storm, do you still find a desire to overcome? Do you refuse to take "no" for an answer? He can take everything you have lost—your time, joy, and integrity—and bring you right up to date as though it never happened.

Give What Remains to God

Samson had lost his integrity, his hair, his strength, his looks, and his eyes. Yet, dying in the enemy's camp, he took what was left and made it available to God. God gave Samson a miracle larger than all the miracles of his entire life.

The disciples had only five barley loaves and two fish, but Jesus asked them to give it to Him. Make what you have available to God, and He will give you a miracle with what is left.

When David faced Goliath, he took off Saul's armor. The shepherd boy had only five stones. He stripped himself of everything else. But David said, "*I come to thee in the name of the Lord of hosts*" (1 Sam. 17:45). He made available to God what he had left.

When the apostle Paul had gone through his storm, the ship was torn to pieces. All he had left was a board, but the board got him safely to the shores of deliverance.

The apostle John didn't have much left. All he had was a testimony, but he made it available to Him who took him higher and gave him a great revelation.

> *After this I looked, and, behold, a door was opened in heaven: and the first voice which I heard was as it were of a trumpet talking with me; which said, Come up hither, and I will shew thee things which must be hereafter* (Revelation 4:1).

The apostle refused to die until he had finished his book.

Some of you have a story to tell, a testimony to give, a book to write. Refuse to die until you have fulfilled your dream. Keep walking with God, for you "*shall not die, but live, and declare the works of the Lord*" (Ps. 118:17).

Be like Enoch. He walked with God in the darkest hour that his time had ever known. It was a time of apostasy and worldliness, but he walked with God. In fact, he walked with God until it was written, *he was not*. God took him higher (Gen. 5:24).

No matter what they say about you, walk with God until they have to say, "He's not what we thought." Let the Holy Spirit reveal to you that there is good stuff left over after all that has happened to you. Strengthen what remains.

Thoughts and Reflections

CHAPTER 8

GOD'S LAYAWAY PLAN

H ow can you keep going when all hell has been unleashed against you? If our generation will usher in the coming of the Lord—and I believe prophecy indicates we will—then we must be equipped to face the onslaught of the devil.

All too often we have heard the story of the gospel, but not the results of the story. Matthew, Mark, Luke, and John tell the story about the gospel. But if we never get past the story, we fail to enter into His fullness.

> *The former treatise have I made, O Theophilus, of all that Jesus began both to do and teach* (Acts 1:1).

This Scripture speaks about what Jesus only began to do. Throughout the epistles we find the ongoing result that the gospel only began to tell.

God Made a Deposit

Of all the epistles that the apostle Paul wrote, one of my favorites is the Book of Ephesians. To really appreciate this letter, you must realize that it was not written from the comforts of a plush motel. Paul penned these words, the first of his prison letters, from the confines of a Roman jail.

Despite his circumstances, Paul viewed life from an eternal perspective.

> *In whom ye also trusted, after that ye heard the word of truth, the gospel of your salvation: in whom also after that ye believed, ye were sealed with that holy Spirit of promise, which is the earnest of our inheritance until the redemption of the purchased possession, unto the praise of his glory* (Ephesians 1:13-14).

The Greek word for earnest is *arrhabon*, meaning a pledge, a down payment, a security deposit. It's an amount paid in advance to secure the transaction until the full price is paid to complete the purchase.

If we see a piece of property that we want but do not have the entire price, we can put a deposit or a down payment on it. Both parties understand that a portion of the payment is still owed. This merely declares to other interested parties that the property already has a purchaser. To confirm the desire to purchase, the potential owner has given earnest money or a security deposit.

If you've ever bought merchandise on layaway, the principle is similar. You place a down payment on your goods with the promise to pay the full amount. At regular intervals you make a payment and take the merchandise home when it has been completely paid off.

Follow the Sequence

Ephesians 1:13-14 shows us that certain things preceded the down payment:

1. *"In whom ye also trusted" (vs. 13).*

This step leads up to the down payment. As we trust Christ as Lord and Savior, we become His purchased possession. A secular company will not put its insignia on a product it does not own. Their logo says, "This is mine. I take responsibility for it." The name seals this possession. It is a declaration of ownership.

2. *"Ye believed" (vs. 13).*

It's one thing to trust when you start out, but it is a far different thing to believe when the odds say it won't happen. You have to trust God even when you can't trace Him. Believe Him when you have no visible evidence. Believe Him when everyone else has given up on you. Believe Him when you are on the mountain, but, more than that, believe Him when the mountain is on you.

It isn't always the one who is shouting and dancing who is the most anointed. The anointing falls on those who have been through the storm and stood the test, who believed through the weeping of the night. The night eventually ends, and a new day will break forth for you.

> *Believe through the weeping unto the new day's dawn.*

3. *"Ye were sealed with that holy Spirit of promise" (vs. 13).*

God will watch to see if you are going to trust Him. Then He will watch to see if by naked faith—without any other visible, tangible manifestation—you are going to believe Him. Then He will seal you, and the seal carries with it a hidden blessing, the Holy Spirit of promise.

God says, "This is Mine, and I promise it will remain Mine through hell and high water because of My seal of approval. This will stand the test. This comes with a lifetime warranty. I seal it." A seal authenticates the vessel and declares, "I own all rights to this vessel. This is good stuff. It has to be because I put My seal of approval upon it."

4. *"Which is the earnest of our inheritance" (vs. 14).*

Notice what the seal stands for in the eyes of God. He wants you enough that He paid earnest money to secure the transaction. When the devil offers you the world,

God says, "Sorry, devil. I began the transaction, and I will finish it! I sealed it with a promise. The transaction will not be complete until I redeem the body. Until that day comes, I own all rights. This is mine."

God Seals on Earth What Heaven Has Decreed in Eternity

God has quickened us, who were once *"dead in trespasses and sins"* (Eph. 2:1). God is eternal, and the life you have is eternal. Many believe they have life but fail to understand they have eternal life. This life is not based upon your merits, but it is based upon His merits. He redeemed or bought you back.

The prefix "re" can be found throughout Scripture. God redeemed you; He reconciled you; He restored you; He regenerated you. Many times God wants us to get to the place where we realize it is all Him and not us.

We Groan Because of What We Know

The apostle Paul used a two-letter word that is packed with dynamite. He mentioned the word "we" eleven times in Second Corinthians 5:18, each time he speaks about the part of you that has received its down payment. The "we" is not the house (our body) because the house will one day die. Because of what "we" know, the "we" in us groans.

The "we" in us is confident; the "we" in us walks; the "we" in us is willing; the "we" in us already knows what is ours. This is why we groan; this is why we walk when it doesn't look like we are going to win.

Notice what keeps the "we" in us going: *"the earnest of the Spirit"* (vs. 5). While we live in this flesh, we are absent from the Lord. But because of the earnest (down payment of the Spirit), we know that one day the mortal part of us will be swallowed up by the life in us.

Even though this primarily speaks of the future resurrection, knowing this can help us conquer our flesh. When our flesh tries to depress or hinder us, saying, "You won't make it," this truth enables our flesh to be swallowed up.

The earnest of the Spirit, which becomes the promise of God's approval upon your life, will swallow up your defeat and anxiety. With this down payment it may not look good right now, but just hold on. You have God's promise.

I can't tell you enough about what this insight will do for you. Because of the earnest of the Spirit, you can always be confident.

Hope Will Change Us

What did the apostle Paul say?

> *And not only they, but ourselves also, which have the firstfruits of the Spirit, even we ourselves groan within ourselves, waiting for the adoption, to wit, the redemption of our body* (Romans 8:23).

The spirit is saved by faith, and the body is saved by hope.

Hope purifies our soul. When it doesn't look good, hope says, "It's all right." This is why we need such a strong witness in our soul. God gives us hope in the midst of our storm.

We must understand the working of the Holy Spirit in our lives. Many become discouraged when they fall short of their goals as a child of God. Others throw in the towel and say, "What's the use?"

Many of you are near a breakthrough in your life. You may have fought for years to get to where you are with God. Many of you are pregnant with destiny. You are carrying within the womb of your spirit a ministry that could change this world.

It's All in a Place

Moses was in the same place where we often find our-selves—near burnout. He had been functioning and abiding in the call of God for his life. Yet he longed for a manifestation of God's presence. Moses prayed:

> *And he said, I beseech thee, shew me thy*
> *glory* (Exodus 33:18).

God wants to show us His glory and splendor as much as, if not more than, we want to see it. In order for us to see the glory of God, however, we must get to the place.

God told Moses:

*And the Lord said, Behold, there is a
place by me, and thou shalt stand upon a
rock* (Exodus 33:21).

Remember, whenever God got ready to manifest
Himself in glory and splendor, He always took the
person up to a mountain or an elevated domain. Then
He would manifest Himself. God promised Moses that
he would see His glory, but only after Moses got to a
certain place. The apostle Peter had a revelation by the
Spirit regarding Christ (Matt. 16:13-18). Jesus was the
Rock, and when we hide ourselves in Him we are taken
to higher heights and deeper depths. A cleft is a small
crevice or opening. When the soldier pierced the side of
Jesus, a cleft opened and we are able, by the Holy Ghost,
to hide in this cleft. God promised Moses:

*I will make all my goodness pass before thee,
and I will proclaim the name of the Lord
before thee.... And it shall come to pass, while
my glory passeth by, that I will put thee in a
clift of the rock, and will cover thee with my
hand while I pass by: And I will take away
mine hand, and thou shalt see my back parts:
but my face shall not be seen* (Exodus 33:19,
22-23).

Moses saw only the afterglow of God's glory, but he
was greatly affected.

The children of Israel saw the face of Moses,
that the skin of Moses' face shone: and Moses
put the vail upon his face (Exodus 34:35).

Some of you are going through a storm, a trial, or something you don't even understand. You're saying to yourself, "I've been faithful. I'm committed to my call. I've exercised my gift, but I still don't understand why this is happening to me."

Don't lose your focus. Help is on the way. What you face will be nothing more than a cleft in the rock. As you go through this problem, you will begin to understand the words of the old hymn, "Rock of Ages, Cleft for Me."

This very storm is taking you to higher ground. Let God raise you to another level through this trial. Noah let a torrential downpour and a flood take him to higher ground. His ark landed upon Mt. Ararat (Gen. 8:14).

You'll Never Be the Same

As Moses spent time on the mountain with God, he began to take on the appearance of God. When Moses came down from the mountain, he had to veil his face to be able to talk with the people. The glory of God was so evident that the people could not look upon him because of the brightness of his countenance.

The apostle Paul asked this question:

> *But if the ministration of death, written and engraven in stones, was glorious, so that the children of Israel could not stedfastly behold the face of Moses for the glory of his countenance; which glory was to be done away: how shall not the ministration of the spirit be rather glorious? For if the ministration of condemnation be glory, much more doth the ministration of righteousness exceed in glory* (2 Corinthians 3:7-9).

The glory of the new covenant and the ministry of righteousness far exceed the ministry of death that came through the law. The apostle Paul closes that chapter with this thought:

> *But we all, with open face beholding as in a glass the glory of the Lord, are changed into the same image from glory to glory, even as by the Spirit of the Lord* (2 Corinthians 3:18).

Open God's Word and allow it to become a mirror. As the Holy Ghost illuminates your life, you will begin to reflect His glory as Moses did. Be willing to pay the price and discipline yourself because God wants to do a work in your life, your ministry, your marriage, and your calling. There is a price to pay to be anointed of God—and an even greater price to maintain your anointing. The Holy Ghost has sealed you, which is a down payment on this great blessing that God is preparing you for. As far as God is concerned, it's done.

Thoughts and Reflections

ABOUT T.D. JAKES

Bishop T.D. Jakes has reached millions of people from all socioeconomic backgrounds, races, nationalities, and creeds. Digital media, film, and television, among others, have been instrumental in helping Bishop Jakes meet the desperate needs of countless individuals. For more than 40 years, Bishop T.D. Jakes has helped millions of people realize their purpose through his dynamic ministry.

Recognized as "America's Best Preacher" by *Time Magazine*, as well as "One of the Nation's Most Influential & Mesmerizing Preachers" by *The New York Times*, Bishop Jakes is a charismatic, yet humble man. In 1996, with minimal resources, T.D. Jakes founded The Potter's House (TPH) in Dallas, Texas, a non-denominational, multicultural church that grew to become a megachurch and global humanitarian organization.

He and his wife, Serita, have been married for more than 35 years and have five children and several grandchildren. Whether enjoying a long, relaxing walk along the beach or launching a business, T.D. and Serita Jakes support each other with their faith in God, and in each other.

OTHER BOOKS
BY T.D. JAKES

Why? Because You Are Anointed

Why? Because You Are Anointed Workbook

Can You Stand to be Blessed?

Woman, Though Art Loosed!

Naked and Not Ashamed

Help Me, I've Fallen and I Can't Get Up!

When Shepherds Bleed

Water in the Wilderness

The Harvest

The Harvest Workbook

The Great Investment

Maximize the Moment

YOUR
Prophetic
C O M M U N I T Y

Are you passionate about hearing God's voice, walking with Jesus, and experiencing the power of the Holy Spirit?

Destiny Image is a community of believers with a passion for equipping and encouraging you to live the prophetic, supernatural life you were created for!

We offer a fresh helping of practical articles, dynamic podcasts, and powerful videos from respected, Spirit-empowered, Christian leaders to fuel the holy fire within you.

Sign up now to get awesome content delivered to your inbox
destinyimage.com/sign-up

 **Destiny Image**